I0412530

# What's the Worst that Could Happen?

# Bad Assumptions, Ignorance, Failures, and Screw-ups

# in Engineering Projects.

Patrick H. Stakem

© November 2012

2nd edition, 2015

ISBN - 9781520207162

# Contents

# Introduction

"Anything that can go wrong, will" attributed to Murphy.

"…at the worst possible time, when you least expect it…" Anon.

"Murphy was an optimist." Anon.

"Never attribute to malice what might instead be only incompetence".

"There is no bad situation that you can't make worse" (attributed to Astronaut Corps)

"You're going down this path, looking left, looking right – something hits you right in the back of the head." Stanley Fischer, Vice Chairman, Federal Reserve Board.

Unfortunately, we learn more from failures than from successes. This book discusses a cross-section of engineering failures, and analyzes them to define the lessons-learned. It also presents some methodologies to prevent failures, or, at least, minimize the effects.

It can be argued that all failures are human failures. We make errors in judgment, we use the wrong model, we solve the wrong problem, we don't verify our solution. There are, of course, natural disasters. These are not our fault, but it can be argued that we need to foresee these and plan an approach. Could the dinosaurs have foreseen the meteor that created the Gulf of Mexico? Not likely. Could the Romans have foreseen the eruption of Vesuvius that destroyed Pompeii? Maybe, with a better world-view. They certainly could have engineered a solution to diverting the lava flow. But what they really needed was a civil defense system with gas masks. Not likely.
The Latin for gas mask is *Nunc larva,* by the way.

This book will present a cross-section of failure studies, mostly drawn from the engineering and aerospace context. Each study includes specific references and a definition of the root cause of the failure. Let's try to learn from other's mistakes. It is less painful to learn from others' failures than your own. We will see errors of omission, errors of commission, and just plain ignorance of the facts.

We will briefly discuss System Engineering processes and procedures that can and should be applied to an architecture before the fact, and, unfortunately, after the fact as a post-mortem analysis. It is important to do a good post-mortem analysis of failures, and document them, for the benefit of the next generation of implementors. This helps to prevent the repeating of mistakes.

There is a huge amount of material on past disasters, mostly descriptive, and without much analysis. Many books could be written on the analysis of past disasters. I necessarily restricted the focus of this book. I didn't include such famous incidents as the Hindenburg disaster, 3-Mile Island, Chernobyl, the Johnstown (PA) Flood, the Great Chicago Fire, the San Francisco Earthquake (many instances), the Dust Bowl Incident of the 1930's in middle America, the Exxon Valdez incident, the Titanic, the Hubble Space Telescope mirror, and many others. I also have not included obvious acts of war and terrorism. With such a wealth of material to cover, I focused on what I thought was interesting and useful in engineering process. Hopefully, this is a good starting point.

Sometimes, even when we are sitting calmly and quietly, a disaster can overcome us, one we did not even cause or influence. Wrong place, wrong time. One the beach when the Tsunami hits, on the edge of the cliff when the earthquake comes, out sailing when the hurricane comes to shore. These are generally termed natural disasters, and they are not our fault. But, we can engineer better predictive and monitoring systems to detect and warn us of impending disasters. Some natural disasters may actually be our fault. Let's be careful. Understand, study, prevent.

I am presenting this mostly from an engineering standpoint, because that is may background. But the concepts apply across all disciplines and endeavors. If your are responsible for a design, a device, a policy, or a program, you must think through the consequences. Always have a plan B. Always think about safety and security. Don't make the same mistake twice. Don't make a second mistake.

Nature and natural systems are not necessarily safe and secure. Let's think avalanche, tsunami, earthquake, volcano … Above and beyond that, systems that are designed and implemented by humans have errors. We can minimize these, but we can't eliminate them. We can study and mitigate the effects of errors, both "accidental" and deliberate.

In 1945, engineers found a moth in the circuitry of the Harvard Mark II computer system, specifically in relay 70 in Panel F. It's dead body blocked the relay from operating correctly, Some attribute the discovery to the "computer" Grace Hopper, later a Navy Admiral, and author of the Cobol language. The poor insect was the origin of the term "computer bug." *Computer* was actually the term for the female attendants of the computing hardware, who, in the absence of able bodied men off at war, did the math and wired the machine to solve a problem. The legend is, the moth was removed and taped in the log book.

This computer legend could certainly be true. I myself had a similar problem where the house air conditioner was cycling on and off rapidly. I found a moth, beaten to death, in the large contactor relay that switched the power to the compressor. I did not tape it in my engineering notebook, though.

I have included a glossary and a list of reference material at the end of the book, and specific references for the failure cases discussed.

Please don't be the clause of a planetary class disaster. Or, at least, please document the case for the benefit of the survivors, to be featured in the next edition of this book.

The author
The author spent 42 years in support of NASA spaceflight mission, on this planet and others. He teaches for the graduate Computer Science Department of Loyola University in Maryland, and for the Johns Hopkins University, Whiting School of Engineering, Engineering for Professionals Program, and

for Capitol Technology University, Engineering and Computer Science Department. He has published some 25 technical books. He is somewhat a hands-on expert with major systems failures.

Second edition
The book was reviewed again after publication, and guess what? More errors were found! Not quite all of these were corrected for the second edition. I also broadened the scope, and included a lot of new material, including some errors. I am interested in hearing about additional failure case studies, and can be contacted at pstakem1@jhu.edu .

# Theory

This section discusses and overview of the system engineering approaches to identify, detect, and preclude failures. It also presents some methodology to analyze why a failure took place, after the fact.

# Expert Opinions

The following are a cross-section of expert opinions, based on experience and keen judgment. You don't always need to heed the advise of experts.

"I think there is a world market for maybe five computers." - Thomas Watson, chairman of IBM, 1943.

"There is no reason anyone would want a computer in their home." - Ken Olson, president, chairman & founder of Digital Equipment Co, 1977.

"This 'telephone' has too many shortcomings to be seriously considered as a means of communication. The device is inherently of no value to us." - Western Union internal memo, 1876.

"The telephone will be used to inform people that a telegram has been sent." - Alexander Graham Bell.

"The wireless music box has no imaginable commercial value. Who would pay for a message sent to nobody in particular?" - David Sarnoff's associates in response to his urgings for investment in the radio in the 1920s.

"Heavier-than-air flying machines are impossible." - Lord Kelvin, president, Royal Society, 1895.

"Professor Goddard does not know the relation between action and reaction and the need to have something better than a vacuum against which to react. He seems to lack the basic knowledge ladled out daily in high schools."- 1921 New York Times editorial about Robert Goddard's revolutionary rocket work.

"The bomb will never go off. I speak as an expert in explosives." - Admiral William Leahy, US Atomic Bomb Project.

"This fellow Charles Lindbergh will never make it. He's doomed." - Harry Guggenheim

"Airplanes are interesting toys but of no military value." - Marechal Ferdinand Foch, Professor of Strategy, Ecole Superieure de Guerre.

"Man will never reach the moon regardless of all future scientific advances." Dr. Lee De Forest, inventor of the vacuum tube.

"Everything that can be invented has been invented." - Charles H. Duell, Commissioner, U.S. Office of Patents, 1899.

"640K (memory) ought to be enough for anybody." - Bill Gates, 1981.

"The transistor is a passing fad."- Dr. William J. Barclay, EE Department, NCSU, 1969.

## Engineering Tools

Various system engineering tools are available to use both before and after "incidents." Ideally, we review the systems before hand with respect to failure and safety, and factor these issues into the implementation plan. Many factors marginalize this approach, including management focus, and impact on systems cost and schedule.

After the fact, we have the Root Cause analysis method, so we can determine what exactly failed, and how this particular issue can be addressed and mitigated. In many cases, this process uncovers other latent issues that also need to be addressed. These need to be documented as case studies for the use of future projects.

## *Root Cause Analysis*

Root Cause Analysis refers to an engineering process to identify and categorize the causes of events, and to identify the primal cause. It is a useful tool for determining why a disaster happened. It is used to define the what, how, and why (and sometimes, who)? Its value is that it will lead to a definition of corrective measures that can be applied in the future.

By definition, root causes are underlying, identifiable, and controllable. The RCA process includes a data collection phase (forensics), a cause charting, the root cause identification, recommendations, and implementation of the solution to avoid repeating the error. In many cases, the RCA will uncover other failure causes that were overlooked.

## *FMEA*

The failure modes and effects analysis is an engineering tool that is applied during the design and testing process of a system. In this approach, we postulate failure modes, and analyze their impact on the system performance. The possible failure modes are examined to confirm their validity. Then, the possible failures are prioritized by severity and consequences. The goal is to identify and eliminate failures in the order of decreasing severity.

The FMEA approach can actually start at the Project conceptual phase, and continue throughout the project life-cycle. It can (and should) be applied to modifications to existing projects. The origins of the FMEA approach were during World War-II, by the U. S. Military. After the war, the approach was adopted by the aviation (aerospace) and automotive industries.

The FMEA analysis requires a cross-functional team, consisting, as applicable of hardware and software engineers, manufacturing, Quality Assurance, test engineers, reliability engineers, parts, and, ideally, the customer.

The process involves identifying the scope of the project, defining the boundaries and the desired level of detail. Then, the system (or project) functions are identified. Each function is analyzed to identify how it could fail. For each of these failure cases, the consequences are noted. These range from no effects to catastrophic. Formally, the consequences are rated on a scale of 1 to 10, with 1 being insignificant to 10, catastrophic. The root cause is then determined for each consequence, starting with the 10's. Software tools are available to support this analysis process.

Once the causes are determined, the controls are defined. Controls prevent the cause from happening, reduce the probability of happening, or detect the failure in time for correction to be applied. For each control, then, a detection probability rating is calculated (or estimated), again on a scale of 1-10. Here, 1 indicates that control is certain, and 10 indicates that the solution will not work. By definition, critical characteristics of the system have a severity of 9 or greater, and have an occurrence and detection rating of greater than 3.

A Risk Priority Number (RPN) is calculated, which is severity times occurrence time detection (ratings). This measure is used to rank failure modes in the order in which they are to be addressed.

Of course, some of these rankings are not measurable, but the result of good engineering guesses

From an FMEA, you can develop contingency plans, adjust to the identified failure scenarios. It is always good to have a Plan B. Also C, D, E......

## Fault Tolerant Design

In this design approach, a system is designed to continue to operate properly in the event of one or more failures. It is sometimes referred to as graceful degradation. There is, of course, a limit to the number of faults or failures than can be handled, and the faults or failures may not be independent. Sometimes, the system will be designed to degrade, but not fail, as a result of the fault. Fault recovery in a fault-tolerate design is either roll forward, or roll back.

Roll back refers to returning the system state to a previous check-pointed state. Roll forward corrects the current system state to allow continuation.

## *Redundancy*

Redundancy refers to the technique of having multiple copies of critical components. Belt and suspenders; two independent ways to accomplish the same results. Either can fail without affecting the other. This can refer to hardware or software. This increases the reliability of the system. Redundant units can be deployed in parallel, such as extra structural members, where each single unit can handle the load. This provides what is referred to as a margin of safety.

In certain systems that are responsible for safety-critical tasks, we might triplicate the critical portion, which, reduces the probability of system failure to small, acceptable, levels. This approach is found in aircraft controls, nuclear power plant controls, and many more, safety-critical systems.

Of course, if there is a common error in the three units, we have not increased our reliability. This situation is referred to as a common mode or single point error. Another problem is in the voting logic, that makes the decision that an error has been made, and switches controllers. At least one satellite launch failed because the voting logic made the wrong choice.

Redundancy carries penalties in size, weight, power, cost, and testing complexity.

Fault isolation allows the system to operate around the failed component, using backup or alternative modules. Fault containment strives to isolate the fault, and prevent propagation of the failure.

One principle of fault tolerant design is replication, with multiple copies of critical systems. Of course, this approach is susceptible to common mode errors. A more vigorous approach is Diversity, where the same task may be accomplished with different implementations. This was the approach chosen for the Shuttle's computers. Generally, a fault detection systems needs to be a separate, independent entity. It's probably of error will be smaller than the main system, because it is simpler. But, it must be closely examined for common mode faults, such as a shared power supply.

Systems can be designed to be fail-safe, fail-soft, or can be "melt-before-fail." The more fault tolerant that is built into a system, the more it will cost, and the more difficult it will be to test. It is important not to increase the complexity to the point where the system is not testable, and is "designed to fail."

## Safety Engineering

Safety Engineering is a systems engineering approach to providing safety in systems, starting from the very beginning, and continuing through the testing phase. Safety Engineering has the goal of preventing hazards and failures.

## Safety Critical Systems

We can all name a lot of safety critical systems such as Nuclear Power Plant control and aircraft systems. But what about the mundane, such as the anti-lock brakes on our cars, or the traffic lights? These we interact with on a daily basis.

# System Failure Case Study's

"Those who cannot learn from history are doomed to repeat it," George Santayana.

This section discusses selected case studies of systems that went wrong, starting in the Aerospace domain. To invoke a baseball analogy, in space, it mostly "one strike and you're out." Not too many second chances are available.

## Common Causes of Space Disasters

There are some common traits we can identify and apply to all system accidents: improper or non-complete requirements, defective architecture or design, complacency about existing safety measures, and management failures.

14

A defective design is the root cause of most space accidents. The nature of the defect is usually obvious in hindsight. The use of a 17 PSI pure oxygen atmosphere during a ground test in case of Apollo 1, the imperfect sealing properties of Shuttle Challenger's solid rocket booster's O-rings are both examples of this.

But a defective design can be identified and corrected before it leads to an accident thanks to quality assurance and analysis of flight parameters during testing and operation of any space hardware. This is where complacency comes into play. Disastrous accidents involving complex systems are always preceded by so-called accident precursors, which take the form of parameters out of tolerance. People responsible for those systems become accustomed to the idea that nothing bad will ever happen because nothing bad has happened yet. A routine inspection of Columbia's ill-fated launch footage performed just a few hours after the launch revealed a foam strike. Mission Control dismissed the strike because the phenomenon had been seen before. The Columbia Accident Investigation Board indeed revealed that every single Shuttle launch presented a certain measure of foam shedding from the External Tank; and even though a precise requirement was set about the tolerance for such foam shedding, the tolerance was simply increased to accommodate the measurements.

It takes a serious management failure to allow a complex organization to become accustomed to the warning signals of a defective design. This failure is often the consequences of pressure to keep up with unrealistic schedules or budgets. When the space Shuttle was first introduced, NASA management claimed it had a reliability of 1 accident in 100,000 flights. After the Challenger Accident, it turned out that the engineering community believed that the reliability was a much more realistically 1 in 100 flights. The engineering community knew about potential issues with the O-rings, but their warnings had not been properly communicated to the management, and even when they did, they were systematically ignored. Every single space disaster, presents a similar set of conditions. That is why we do a post mortem analysis. Hindsight is often 20/20.

## Aerospace

Getting spacecraft off the surface of the planet and into orbit, or to other planets is somewhat difficult. There are many documented failure cases in this realm, not because the rocket scientists and engineers make more mistakes, but due to the difficulty of the endeavor. This is an area of particular interest to me, as I worked as a NASA support contractor since the 1970's on many missions. I have a lot of case studies in this area. A much more exhaustive study in the area is the book by Harland and Lorenz, dated 2005, which is in the reference section at the end of this book. There is a lot more material that happened since 2005, unfortunately.

The author is coming from an aerospace background, and has seen first hand the increased difficulties of getting stuff to orbit, and getting it back safely.

When I was at the West Coast launch site at Vandenberg AFB, I was waiting for the top level service platform to clear so I could go up to check the payload. I was relaxing at the base, leaning up against one of the solid strap-on boosters of the Delta launch vehicle, chatting with one of the pad techs. I asked the tech causally what would happen if the booster erroneously ignited. He said to ignore that, we would never know.

I took a series of safety training courses for launch pad 39 access at Cape Kennedy, in the Shuttle era. Liquids onboard rockets tend to be universally dangerous, present in large quantities, and pressurized. There is a lot that can kill you, and not just by explosion and fire. My all-time favorite was red fuming nitric acid. If it leaks, it forms a reddish brown cloud, hugging the ground. You need to run at right angles to the way that cloud is moving. If you get caught up in it, they may find your belt buckle, but heavily corroded.

## *Launch Vehicle Reliability*

The first tricky part is getting the payload off the ground. This has been shown to be a hazardous task since the initial work by Von Braun in Germany, and Robert Goddard, in the U. S. Let's keep in mind that Robert Goddard was supposedly asked to stop his rocket launches by the Fire Marshall. If the launch vehicle fails, the payload is irrelevant. We'll look at a few launch vehicle failures.

# Titan Launch Vehicle

The Titan missile was a mainstay of the ballistic missile deterrent system during the Cold War. Housed in hardened underground bunkers, the missiles were fueled and ready to retaliate against any nation attacking the United States. They were dispersed geographically across the country. Later, the Titan was used as a space launch vehicle for both military and civilian missions. A Titan missile was never launched in anger, or retaliation. But, at least once, it did launch a nuclear warhead.

In 1980, at a Titan II missile silo in Arkansas, a maintenance technician dropped a wrench that fell 70 feet, and punctured the skin of the missile. Leaking rocket fuel ignited and blew the 8,000 lb nuclear warhead out of the silo. It landed harmlessly several hundred feet away. However, 1,400 people in a five mile radius, were told to run. That was going to do a lot of good.

What's are the issues here? Why weren't the wrenches tethered, so they couldn't be dropped? Did any one calculate the probability of puncturing the missile skin by a dropped object? Did anyone calculate the probability of the puncture that caused a leak and subsequent fire and explosion? The one good thing we can say is that the nuclear weapons design team did an exemplary good job in designing fail-safes into the trigger mechanism. After all, what's the worst that could happen? If our enemies can't set off a nuclear weapon in Arkansas, we should at least make sure we can't either.

In 1985, a Titan-3D launch vehicle exploded after liftoff from Vandenburg AFB in California. This was the first failure in 12 years. In 1986, another Titan exploded shortly after launch at the same location, Then, a Delta launch vehicle carrying a weather satellite exploded after liftoff from Cape Canaveral. With the Shuttle Challenger disaster, this effectively put a stop to payloads going to orbit for the U. S. An unintended consequence of the grounding of the rocket fleet was that excess solid propellant was stored at the manufacturing plant in Nevada. The plant managed to catch fire, and exploded, destroying the facility.

In 1999, a Titan IV-B with a Centaur upper stage and Milstar satellite left Cape Canaveral Air Station, bound for geosynchronous orbit. After the

Centaur second stage with the payload separated from the Titan booster at 9 minutes into the flight, things started to go wrong. Instability in the roll axis became pitch and yaw axis instability which became uncontrolled tumbling. The Centaur struggled to control these errors, but depleted its available propellant. The Milstar payload ended up in the wrong orbit. The mission was declared a complete loss by the Secretary of the Air Force, with a cost of around one billion dollars. This was the third straight failure of a Titan mission, and got extensive interest from the Media.

The Accident Investigation Board reach the conclusion that the problem was due to a "failed software development, testing, and quality assurance process." Human error was the cause of an incorrect entry of a value for the roll rate filter constant. This was seen during testing, but not recognized as an error, the consequences were not appreciated, and the error was not corrected. The software development process was shown to allow single point failures. The Independent Verification and Validation (IV&V) Process was not applied to the roll rate filter constant.

Reference

*sunnyday.mit.edu/**accidents/titan**_1999_rpt.doc*

http://www.spacedaily.com/news/titan-99e.html

http://www.youtube.com/watch?v=ZFeZkrRE9wI

## *Ariane 5*

The European Ariane 5 launch vehicle was a follow-on to, and improvement of the Ariane-4. These were launched from a site in French Guiana near the Equator, to take maximum advantage of the Earth's rotation. Ariane 5's first test flight (Flight 501) in June, 1996 failed, with the rocket self-destructing 37 seconds after launch because of a malfunction in the control software. A data conversion from 64-bit floating point value to 16-bit signed integer value to be stored in a variable representing horizontal bias caused a processor trap (operand error) because the floating point value was too large to be represented by a 16-bit signed integer. The software was originally written for the Ariane 4 where efficiency considerations (the computer running the software had an 80% maximum workload requirement) led to 4 variables being protected with a handler while 3 others, including the horizontal bias variable, were left unprotected because it was thought that they were "physically limited or that there was a large margin of error". The software, written in Ada, was included in the Ariane 5 through the reuse of an entire Ariane 4 subsystem despite the fact that the particular software containing the bug, which was just a part of the subsystem, was not required by the Ariane 5 because it has a different preparation sequence than the Ariane 4. The incident resulted in a loss of over $500 million. The launch vehicle and its payload were scattered across square kilometers of mangrove swamp.

The Root Cause was a flight control system failure. Not a hardware error, but a software error, more of a math error. A diagnostic code from failed (Inertial Reference System) IRS-2 was interpreted as data. IRS-1 had failed earlier. The diagnostic data was sent because of a software error. The software module was only supposed to be used for alignment, not during flight. The diagnostic code was considered as a 64-bit floating point number, and converted to a 16-bit signed integer, but the value was too large to fit in 16 bits. This caused the rocket nozzles to steer hard-over to the side, causing the vehicle to veer off course and crash.

References

De Dalmau, J. and Gigou J. "Ariane-5: Learning from flight 501 and Preparing for 502, http://esapub.esrin.esa.it/bulletin/bullet89/dalma89.html

Lions, Prof, J. L. (Chairman) ARIANE 5 flight 501 Failure, Report by the Inquiry Board, 19 July 1996, http://www.esrin.esa.it/tidc/htdocs/Press/Press96/ariane5rep.html

Jezequel, Jean-marc and Meyer, Bertrand "Design by Contract: The Lessons of Ariane," IEEE computer, Jan. 1997, vol 30, n. 2, pp129-130.

"Inquiry Board Traces Ariane 5 Failure to Overflow Error,"
http://siam.org/siamnews/general/ariance.html

Baber, Robert L. "The Ariane 5 explosion as seen by a software engineer,"
http://www.cs.wits.ac.za/~bob/ariane5.htm

## Patriot Missile

The MIM-104 Patriot surface to air missile system replaced the earlier Nike-Hercules and Hawk missile systems for air defense. Anti-missile defense was a fledgling concept at the time. It had been demonstrated in test conditions, but a hostile missile had never been intercepted in combat. It got its trail by fire in the First Gulf War, engaging around 40 incoming SCUD ballistic missiles. It was calculated that the Patriot had a 70% success rate in interceptions. It's the 30% failure rate that we focus on. In general, multiple Patriots were launched against each incoming missile.

The Iraqi SCUD (Al-Hussein) was a Russian design, modified by the Iraqis to lighten the missile to increase its range and speed. In the process, they managed to make the missile unstable in flight. It is a tactical ballistic missile, launched from its own mobile transporter-erector. Scuds had first been launched against Iran by Iraq in 1982, and Iran responded in kind, and hit Baghdad. The Iraqi missiles could not hit Tehran in Iran, hence the range-extension project. They eventually managed to hit Tehran with 135 missiles, causing the capitol to be evacuated.

During the First Gulf War, on February 25, 1991, an American Patriot antimissile battery failed to intercept an incoming Iraqi Scud ballistic missile. The subsequent missile strike killed 28 American soldiers of the 14th Quartermaster Detachment in a barracks at Dhahran. Wrong place, wrong time.

The Patriot was designed to be an anti-aircraft and anti-missile defense weapon. It used Phased Array Tracking and Distance radar to monitor incoming threats, and sent tracking intercept steering commands to the missiles in flight.

The Root Cause of the failure to intercept was a timing inaccuracy due to excessive clock drift. This lead to incorrect intercept information. The missile battery had been active for over 100 hours, causing excessive clock drift. This resulted in an error of 0.3433 seconds, corresponding to a distance traveled by the SCUD missile of half a kilometer.

The Patriot was not designed to be active for long periods of time, and the calculation error had not been detected in testing. The Israelis were aware of the problem, and had notified the Army. There was not a software fix ready, but they recommended rebooting the system on a regular basis. Cntrl-Alt-Del.

Reference

*Patriot Missile Defense, Software Problem Led to System Failure at Dharan, Saudi Arabia*, Feb 1992, U.S. Government General Accounting Office, GAO/IMTEC-92-25.

## *Proton Launch Vehicle*

A Proton-M rocket launched Russia's Ekspress-AM4 communications satellite. The launch vehicle completed its mission successfully, but the payload failed to deploy into a geosynchronous transfer orbit after it was reported to have lost all power around the time of the fourth burn.

An investigation determined that the failure had been caused by a blocked oxidizer line, and action was taken to prevent a recurrence. Two years later, in March 2008, an identical failure occurred during the launch of AMC-14. In this case the Briz-M upper stage shut down 133 seconds before the end of a 32 minute burn. Another investigation was conducted, and it was discovered that a gas duct had ruptured due to a combination of overheating, pressure fluctuations during the long burn, and erosion.

The earlier Proton-K initially had exceptionally poor reliability: in 1969 alone it suffered eight launch failures from ten attempts.

## Sea Launch

The SeaLaunch service provides a launch platform on the equator to maximize the benefit of the Earth's rotation, much like the ESA launch site in French Guiana. It uses repurposed Ukrainian Zenit ballistic missiles as the launch vehicle. It is an International commercial, non-government organization. The major payloads for Sealaunch services are commercial communication satellites going to geosynchronous orbit.

Launches are conducted from the Ocean Odyssey platform, at 154 degrees west longitude. The rockets and payloads are integrated in Long Beach, California, and taken by the ship Sea Launch Commander to the launch site. A fully automated 3-day countdown process is used.

Of some 35 rockets launched, there have been three total failures, and one recoverable failure, where a payload went to the wrong orbit, but this was later corrected.

The first failure was during the third flight, in 2000, where a software error resulted in the early cut-off of the second stage engine, resulting in the payload's failure to reach orbit. This was later shown to be a code review and test problem, that did not catch the error. The root cause was the omission of a ground software command to close a second stage valve, prior to launch.

In 2004, the upper stage shut down prematurely due to a wiring fault, putting the payload in a lower orbit than desired. The payload was able to reach the desired orbit at the cost of using its own fuel, intended for on-orbit station-keeping.

In January 2007, the Zenit launch vehicle exploded on the launch pad after an engine failure caused by debris in the turbo-pump assembly. This caused considerable damage to the launch platform.

In February 2013, the Zenit launch vehicle suffered a premature engine shutdown, and the rocket plunged into the Pacific Ocean shortly after launch.

References

Zenit-3SL. *Launch Vehicles*. National Space Agency of Ukraine, http://www.nkau.-gov.ua/nsau/

"Rocket carrying US satellite plunges into Pacific Ocean 40 seconds after launch". Daily Mail. 2013-02-01.

## Nedelin

The Nedelin catastrophe was a launch pad accident that occurred on in October 1960 at the Baikonur launch site during the test of a Soviet R-16 ICBM. As a prototype of the missile was being prepared for a test flight, an explosion occurred. Second stage engines ignited accidentally, killing many military and technical personnel working on the preparations. Despite the magnitude of the disaster, news of it was suppressed for many years. The Soviet government did not acknowledge the event until 1989. The disaster is named after the commanding officer of the Soviet Union's Strategic Rocket Forces, Nedelin. He was also head of the R-16 development program.

On 23 October, the prototype R-16 was installed on launching pad 41 awaiting final tests before launch. The missile was over 30 m long, 3.0 m in diameter and had a launch weight of 141 tons. The rocket was fueled with "Devil's Venom." This was the Russian term for hypergolic UDMH as the fuel and a saturated solution of di-nitrogen tetroxide in nitric acid as the oxidizer. These were used forthe high boiling point and storability. They are both extremely corrosive and toxic. These risks were accounted for in the safety requirements of the launch procedures, but Nedelin's insistence on performing tests before the November 7th anniversary of the Bolshevik Revolution resulted in extreme schedule pressure, with numerous safety procedures being ignored in order to save time.

A short circuit in a main sequencer caused the second stage engines, while being tested before launch, to fire inadvertently. This detonated the first-stage fuel tanks directly below, destroying the missile in an enormous explosion. Automatic cameras set around the launching pad filmed the explosion in detail. People near the rocket were instantly incinerated; those farther away were burned to death or poisoned by the toxic fuel component vapors. As soon as the engines  fired, most of the personnel ran to the perimeter but were trapped inside the security fence and  engulfed in a fireball. The resultant explosion incinerated Nedelin, a top aide, the USSR's top missile guidance designer, and seventy-one other officers and engineers. Missile designer Mikhail Yangel  survived only because he had left to smoke a cigarette behind a bunker a few hundred yards away. A case of cigarette smoking being good for your health.

Complete secrecy was immediately imposed on the events by Nikita Khrushchev. A news release said Nedelin had died in a plane crash and the families of the other engineers were "advised" to say their loved ones had died of the same cause. Khrushchev also ordered Leonid Brezhnev to head an investigation commission. Among other things, the commission found that many more people were present on the launch pad than should have been. According to Sergei Khrushchev, Brezhnev insisted that the commission punish no one, explaining that "The guilty have already been punished."

After the committee presented its report, the R-16 program resumed in January 1961 with a first successful flight in November. The delay to the R-16 spurred the USSR toward the development of more effective ICBMs and sparked Khrushchev's decision to install IRBMs in Cuba.

A memorial to the victims of the testers was erected in the first half of the 1960s in the Park of Baikonur and is still visited by  officials before any manned launch

In 1980, a Vostok-2M rocket (derived from the R-7 ICBM and man-rated) exploded on its launch pad at Plesetsk during a fueling operation, killing 48 people. An investigation into a similar– but avoided– accident revealed that the substitution of lead-based for tin-based solder in hydrogen peroxide filters allowed the breakdown of the hydrogen peroxide, causing the resultant explosion.

In 1996, a Chinese Long March launch vehicle veered off course seconds after launch, killing a large number of people. In1995, a Long March 2E rocket veered off course two seconds after take-off from the Xichang Space Center and exploded, killing at least six on the ground. On February 14, 1996, a similar failure occurred during the launch of Intelsat 708: The rocket veered severely off course immediately after clearing the launch tower and crashed into a village. Officials later blamed the failure on an "unexpected gust of wind."

ref:

http://www.youtube.com/watch?v=FBJ9ue6GKek

You get the point? Rockets are dangerous. Whether you're just standing around, or riding one.

## *Gemini*

Gemini 8 was the 1966 sixth manned spaceflight in NASA's Gemini program, carrying two men onboard. The mission conducted the first docking of two spacecraft in orbit, but also suffered the first critical in-space system failure of a U.S. spacecraft which threatened the lives of the astronauts and required immediate abort of the mission. The crew was returned to Earth safely. The only other time this happened was on the flight of Apollo 13.

There was some suspicion on the ground that the Agena target's attitude control system was acting up and might not have the correct program. Shortly before radio blackout with the ground, Mission Control cautioned the astronauts to immediately abort the docking if any abnormalities occurred with the Agena.

After the Agena began execution of its stored command program, which instructed the Agena to turn the combined spacecraft 90° to the right, Astronaut Scott noticed that they were in a roll. Armstrong used the Gemini's OAMS thrusters to stop the roll, but it immediately started again. Gemini 8 was out of range of ground communications at this time.

Armstrong saw that the OAMS fuel had dropped to 30%, indicating that the problem could be on their own spacecraft. With concern that the high spin rate might damage one or both spacecraft or even lead to the propellant-heavy Agena rupturing or exploding, they decided to undock from the Agena to analyze the situation. Scott switched the Agena control back to ground command, while Armstrong struggled to stabilize the combined vehicle enough to permit undocking. Scott then hit the undock button, and Armstrong fired a long burst of translation thrusters to back away from the Agena.

Without the added mass of the Agena, the Gemini's rate of spin began to increase quickly. Soon after this, they came in range of a ground communications ship. The spin rate had reached one revolution per second, causing the astronauts' vision to become blurred and putting them in danger of losing consciousness or suffering vertigo. Armstrong decided to shut down the OAMS and used the Re-entry Control System (RCS) thrusters to stop the spin. After steadying the spacecraft, they tested each OAMS thruster in turn and found that Number 8 had stuck on. Almost 75% of the reentry maneuvering fuel had been used to stop the spin, and mission rules dictated that the flight be aborted once the RCS was fired for any reason. Gemini 8 immediately prepared for an emergency landing.

No conclusive reason for the thruster malfunction was ever found. The most probable cause was determined to be an electrical short, most likely due to a static electricity discharge. Power still flowed to the thruster, even when it was switched off. To prevent recurrence of this problem, the design  was changed so each thruster had its own  isolated circuit.

There were spacesuit design flaws noted on the later Gemini 9 mission. On the third day, Astronaut Cernan began his EVA, which proved to be troubled from the start. After pumping up his pressure suit to three and one half pounds of pressure per square inch, "the suit took on a life of its own and became so stiff that it didn't want to bend at all." He struggled to move inside his stiff suit As soon as he left the spacecraft, he began tumbling uncontrollably, which was not helped by his stiff umbilical which gave Cernan difficultly in controlling his movements. He eventually made it back to the hatch area. After trying to remove a mirror mounted to the side of the spacecraft, his suit cooling system overheated and his face plate fogged up completely, denying him any vision.

Co-astronaut on the mission Stafford said in a 2001 interview that there was a real concern that Cernan would not be able to get back into the capsule. As it would not have been acceptable for Stafford to cut Cernan loose in orbit, he stated that the plan was to make re-entry with the astronaut still attached by his umbilical. However, such an action would have resulted in the deaths of both men.

## *Apollo*

The story of the Apollo-13 mission is well known, and will not be covered here. See the movie. But an interesting situation had occurred earlier to Neil Armstrong, before he got to be the first man to step on the moon.

On May 6, 1968, more than a year before his moon landing, Armstrong had a narrow escape in the lunar landing research vehicle (LLRV) at Ellington Air Force Base. On a simulated lunar descent, leaking propellant caused a total failure of his flight controls and forced an ejection. His only injury was a hard tongue bite. In his biography, *First Man*, author James Hansen recounts how astronaut Alan Bean saw Armstrong that afternoon at his desk in the astronaut office. Bean then heard colleagues in the hall talking about the accident, and asked them, "When did this happen?" About an hour ago, they replied. Bean returned to Armstrong and said, "I just heard the funniest story!" Armstrong said, "What?" "I heard that you bailed out of the LLTV an hour ago." "Yeah, I did," replied Armstrong. "I lost control and had to bail out of the darn thing." "I can't think of another person," Bean recalls, "let alone another astronaut, who would have just gone back to his office after ejecting a fraction of a second before getting killed."

Reference:

Lunar Landing Training Vehicle No. 1 Accident Investigation Board Report December 8, 1968. NASA. March 12 1969.

Lunar Landing Training Vehicle No. 2 Accident Investigation Board Report January 29, 1971. NASA March 18 1971.

Report by the NASA Accident Review Board on the Flight Accident with LLRV #1 on May 6, 1968. NASA. July 12, 1968.

(https://nsc.nasa.gov/SFCS/SystemFailureCaseStudy/Details/155)

Apollo Soyuz

Apollo-Soyuz was a joint project between the two spacefaring nations in 1975. The author supported the mission by keeping the communications relay satellite ATS-6 pointed correctly for live television relay from the vehicles. The ATS-6 relay satellite had developed a pointing problem in its onboard computer, that alluded us for a few weeks.

Upon reentry, the Apollo crew were accidentally exposed to toxic nitrogen tetroxide fumes, caused by the reaction control system (RCS) oxidizer venting from the spacecraft and entering a cabin air intake. The RCS was inadvertently left on during descent, and the highly toxic nitrogen tetroxide was sucked into the spacecraft as it drew in outside air. Astronaut Brand briefly lost consciousness Stafford retrieved emergency oxygen masks, put one on Brand, and gave one to Slayton. The three astronauts were hospitalized for two weeks in Honolulu. Brand took responsibility for the mishap; because of high noise levels in the cabin during reentry, he believes he was unable to hear Stafford call off one item of the reentry checklist, the closure of two switches which would have automatically shut off the RCS and initiated drogue parachute deployment.

## *Fire in Space*

There have been several instances of fire in a manned spacecraft. The tragic Apollo-1 fire during a launch rehearsal at the Kennedy Space Center killed the three astronauts. Part of the problem was the 100% oxygen atmosphere withing the capsule, as well as the presence of flammable materials. This lead to the deaths of three skilled and dedicated astronauts. Ed White, Roger Chafee, and Gus Grissom. Cosmonaut candidate Valentin Bondarenko was killed in a fire during a training exercise in an oxygen-rich isolation chamber" in 1961.

The test was considered to be non-hazardous because neither the launch vehicle nor the spacecraft was loaded with fuel or cryogenics, and all pyrotechnic systems were disabled. The spacecraft's fuel cell reactants were not loaded for this test. Only the solid fuel rockets in the escape system posed any potential danger.

The Astronauts were in continuous contact with the Operations and Control building. Astronaut White reported, "I've got a fire in the cockpit!" The hull of the capsule ruptured within seconds. It was not possible for the astronauts to open the hatch. It took the pad crew 5 minutes to open the hatch from the outside, only to find a horrific scene.

An inward opening hatch had been specified by NASA, based on previous problems with the outward opening hatch of Mercury, which caused the loss of the capsule on Gus Grissom's flight. The hatch could not have possibly been opened inwardly against the estimated 29 psi, generated by the combustion.

NASA grounded all manned flight, and there was a Congressional Investigation. Among other changes, the pure oxygen atmosphere was abandoned in favor of a 60% oxygen, 40 % nitrogen at at sea level pressure at launch, vented down to 5 psi in orbit. The astronaut's suits were left with a pure oxygen atmosphere to avoid the bends, the same problems that divers have when ascending too quickly from depth. They launched with closed helmets, and removed these once on orbit. The new spacecraft had an outward opening hatch. All cabin materials were reviewed, and only non-flammable materials were allowed.

Gus Grissom and Roger Chaffee were buried at Arlington National Cemetery, and Ed White was buried at West Point Cemetery.

Reference: http://history.nasa.gov/Apollo204/phillip1.html

The Space Mirror, or Astronaut Memorial is located at the Kennedy Space Center. It was dedicated in 1991 to remember the lives of the men and women who have died in the various space programs of the United States.

http://www.astronautmemorial.net/

Besides twenty NASA career astronauts, the memorial includes the names of a U.S. Air Force X-15 test pilot, a U.S. Air Force officer who died while training for a then-classified military space program, a civilian spaceflight participant who died in the Challenger disaster, and an Israeli astronaut who was killed during the Columbia disaster.

The memorial was designed to track the Sun across the sky in pan and tilt. In accordance with the theme of this book, the sun tracking system failed, allowing part of the monument to strike a steel beam on an adjacent platform. It was repaired but the mechanism later again ground to a halt. It was not subsequently repaired.

The Cosmonaut Memorial is located in Moscow.

A Russian Progress resupply vehicle accidentally rammed the MIR space station, breaching the Spektr module and causing a dangerous depressurization. The Mir-23 crew worked quickly to save the station. American Astronaut Michael Foale had arrived at Mir via the shuttle Atlantis, on mission STS-84.

The Progress collided with a solar array on the Spektr module. Then, the spacecraft hit Spektr itself, punched a hole in a solar panel, buckled a radiator, and breached the integrity of Spektr's pressure hull. The crew heard hissing and their ears began popping. Then the decompression alarm system went off.

The power outage only lasted about a day-and-a-half. Because of the orientation of Mir's orbit at that time, the station was more often in Earth's shadowt. Only when a panel happened to be in direst sunlight did they have enough power to contact ground controllers in Moscow.

The collision had knocked Mir into a spin; and the power outage had shut down the gyros so that the spin went uncontrolled. To stop the spin and face the arrays toward the Sun, the crew needed to know the spin rate of Mir. However, the computer and other instruments were out of operation. So, in the dark and in the silence, Foale went to the windows in the airlock and held his thumb up to the field of stars. Combining a sailor's technique with hiss knowledge of physics, Foale estimated the spin rate of the space station. Then, he and Lazutkin radioed the estimates down to the Moscow Control Center. The ground controllers fired Mir's engines, and stopped the spin.

With all the power outages, a lot of condensate had built up on Mir's interior surfaces. According to Foale, "Fifty percent of my time was spent just mopping up water. It was like cave diving, going into a dark module with a full-length suit on." Foale mopped up the water with old underwear, used clothes, or with a device that sucked the water into an airtight bag.

Foale's crewmates told him about the troubles during Astronaut Linenger's previous visit to Mir, which including the fire.

Reference - http://history.nasa.gov/SP-4225/nasa5/nasa5.htm

## Space Transportation System

There were several "minor" Shuttle problems before two of the units were lost in tragic circumstances. Let's be clear – there is no minor problem on a manned mission.

In 1984, Shuttle Discovery on mission STS-41 had a valve problem in main engine number 3 at T-4 seconds. This was successfully detected, and the engines were shut down successfully. The crew was removed, and the vehicle stack was returned to the Vertical Assembly Building for repair.

In 1985, Challenger on STS-51 had a coolant valve problem on a main engine detected at T-3. The engines were shut down, and the valve was replaced on the pad. Another problem surfaced on the subsequent launch, when a faulty sensor shut down main engine number 1 early. The vehicle continued to orbit, a bit lower than planned.

Shuttle Columbia on STS-55 in 1993 had a problem with main engine number two. All three engines were replaced on the pad, and the subsequent launch went fine. Shuttle Discovery, on STS-51 in 1993, had a problem detected at T-3, where the sensor monitoring liquid hydrogen fuel flow in main engine number 2 failed. Again, all the engines were changed out on the pad.

In 1994, Shuttle Endeavor, on mission STS-68, had a problem occur at T-1 (second), where a sensor was higher than acceptable readings for the exhaust temperature of the high pressure oxygen turbopump of main engine number 3. In this case, the vehicle was rolled back to the Vertical Assembly Building to replace all three engines. The faulty engine was sent to the Stennis Space Center for rework, and showed a fuel flow metering sensor problem, which lead to the problem seen.

The Space Shuttle Main Engines were modular, and refurbished and reused on subsequent flights. They were interchangeable among Shuttles as well.

## Shuttle Abort Modes

The Shuttle main engines, burning liquid hydrogen and liquid oxygen, were ignited sequentially, with about a one second delay, and each was evaluated for correct thrust. Even with all three engines going, the vehicle would not leave the pad without the massive thrust of the solid main engines (and the release of the explosive bolts, holding it to the pad.) Problesm were detected, and the main engines were shut down successfully five times during the Shuttle Program. The Astronauts reported the nose of the Orbiter vehicle swung forward about a meter, when the three main engines were ignited but the vehicle constrained, and swung back when the solids were lit. This was called the "twang."

Once the explosive bolts were fired, and the solid boosters were ignited, the Shuttle was going...somewhere. If a problem was detected now, there were a series of abort modes pre-defined. There were the result of extensive engineering analysis of what could go wrong, and how to mitigate the situation.

There were two basic abort modes, abort to orbit, and abort to a landing sight. It depended on whether one or both solids were faulty. Low orbit could actually be achieved with one solid booster, with the main engines countering the asymmetrical thrust. Other possible reasons for an abort could come from multiple APU failure, a cabin pressurization problem, or as leak in the fuel tank.

The shuttle could possibly do a return to launch site abort, using some of the solid boosters thrust to turn and head back to the launch site. The tricky part was using up the remaining fuel in the external tank before jettisoning. The shuttle would then land at the runway at Kennedy Space Center. This event was never necessary. The return to launch site abort was described by Astronaut Mullane as "an unnatural act of Physics." It required careful pre-planning and execution to manage energy, and to not exceed structural load limits on the vehicle. After about 4 minutes after lift-off, a return to launch site was no longer possible, and the Transoceanic Abort Landing would be used. This used pre-designated airfields in Africa or Europe. This mode was also never needed during the program.

Next in line was the Abort-once-around. Here, the Shuttle returned to the Kennedy runway after one orbit of the Earth. Next was the Abort to orbit (just not the right orbit). This contingency was used during STS-51, due to a solid booster problem. The mission continued successfully.

## Shuttle Challenger Disaster

In January 1986, the Space Shuttle Challenger broke up some 73 seconds into its flight, killing the seven crew members, and destroying the vehicle and payload. About 17 % of the U. S. population watched this live on television. I had a classmate on that flight.

It happened to be extremely cold at the launch site, cold enough for ice to form on the launch towers. A major discussion ensued between NASA management and contractor Morton Thiokol about the engine seals not being qualified at those temperatures. The decision to launch was eventually made. One thing to keep in mind is that management decisions do not repeal the laws of physics.

The o-rings were so hard at launch time they could not properly seal the gap between engine sections, and were vaporized. However, material from the burn temporarily sealed the gap. This material was broken up later due to aerodynamic forces, and flame from the solid engine hit the hydrogen main engine tank. The crew cabin survived the explosion, and went into free-fall. It impacted into the ocean at over 200 mph, not a survivable event. The debris was spread across a large area of deep water.

As a result of the Shuttle problems, the U.S. Air Force abandoned the Shuttle as a carrier for classified payloads.

The disaster caused a 32-month delay in the launch of the next mission, and President Regan appointed the Rogers Commission to find and correct the problem. The commission assigned blame to NASA's organization culture and decision-making processes There were also Congressional investigations.

During one of these, a long discussion took place over whether the seals between the solid booster segments were affected by the cold, with strong engineering opinions on each side. Finally, noted physicist Richard Feynman dropped a sample of the material into his glass of ice water, took it out later and dropped it on the table, where it broke. The discussion was concluded. Feynman got his own Appendix to the official report.

Feynman included his observation, ""For a successful technology, reality must take precedence over public relations, for nature cannot be fooled."

The overall Committee Report said, "...the Committee feels that the underlying problem which led to the Challenger accident was not poor communication or underlying procedures as implied by the Rogers Commission conclusion. Rather, the fundamental problem was poor technical decision-making over a period of several years by top NASA and contractor personnel, who failed to act decisively to solve the increasingly serious anomalies in the Solid Rocket Booster joints."

After the Reports were issued, NASA conducted a total review and redesign of the solid rocket boosters, with independent oversight. NASA also opened an Office of Safety, Reliability, and Quality Assurance.

"Why no ejection seats?" has been asked. The first couple of test flights did have them, but the Shuttle crew became larger, and not all were on the flight (upper) deck for launch. The problem was how to get the Mission Specialist Astronauts off the middeck. Another issue, as defined by Astronaut Bob Crippen, was "...if you had to use them while the solids were there, I don't believe you'd—if you popped out and then went down through the fire trail that's behind the solids, that you would have ever survived, or if you did, you wouldn't have a parachute, because it would have been burned up in the process. But by the time the solids had burned out, you were up to too high an altitude to use it. ... So I personally didn't feel that the ejection seats were really going to help us out if we really ran into a contingency."

Reference

Robert L. Crippen", NASA Johnson Space Center Oral History Project, 26 May 2006.

*Report of the PRESIDENTIAL COMMISSION on the Space Shuttle Challenger Accident*, June 6th, 1986, Washington, D.C; Report to the President, IMPLEMENTATION OF THE RECOMMENDATIONS of the

Presidential Commission on the Space Shuttle Challenger Accident June 1987, updated Dec. 8, 2010, (available history.nasa.gov)

## Shuttle Columbia Disaster

The Space shuttle Columbia, OV-102, flew the first Shuttle mission in 1981, and completed 27 successful missions. It disintegrated during reentry on its 28th mission, STS-107, in 2003, and the seven crew members died. Columbia had spent 16 days in orbit. The resulting debris field stretched across hundreds of miles of Texas and into Louisiana. Members of the Texas Forest Service and a helicopter pilot lost their lives in an accident during the recovery operations.

The cause was determined to be a hole in the leading edge of a wing, formed when a chunk of insulating foam from the external tank had broken off and impacted the wing during launch. Such damage had evidently been observed before, and fixed after landing, but was never thought to be a major concern. In the case of Columbia, the leading edge of the wing was damaged enough to allow super hot gas to enter the wing, causing extensive damage to structure, controls, and wiring.

The Columbia Accident Investigation Board concluded that NASA had not learned enough or applied the knowledge from the Challenger accident. Lessons Learned were not heeded. They blamed "the same flawed decision making process that had resulted in the *Challenger* accident" for Columbia's destruction.

Columbia Point, a mountain in Colorado was named for the Mission. It is located about a half-mile from Challenger Point, in the Sangre de Christo mountain range.

References

Columbia Crew Survival Investigation Report, NASA/SP-2008-565, http://www.nasa.gov/pdf/298870main_SP-2008-565.pdf

## Shuttle Atlantis

On mission STS-27, Atlantis' Thermal Protection System tiles sustained extensive damage during the flight. Ablative insulating material from the right-hand solid rocket booster nose cap had hit the orbiter about 85 seconds into the flight, as seen in footage of the ascent. The STS-27 crew also commented that white material was observed on the windshield at various times during ascent. The crew made an inspection of the shuttle's impacted starboard side using the shuttle's robot arm, but the limited resolution and range of the cameras made it impossible to determine the full extent of the tile damage.

The problem was compounded by the fact that the crew was prohibited from using their standard method of sending images to ground control due to the classified nature of the mission. The crew was forced to use a slow, encrypted transmission method, likely causing the images NASA engineers received to be of poor quality, causing them to think the damage was actually "just lights and shadows". They told the crew the damage did not look any more severe than on past missions.

One report describes the crew as "infuriated" that Mission Control seemed unconcerned. Commander Gibson did not believe that the Shuttle could survive reentry; if instruments indicated that the shuttle was disintegrating, he planned to "tell mission control what I thought of their analysis" in the remaining seconds before his death. Fortunately, Atlantis landed without incident. The magnitude of the damage was significant. Over 700 damaged tiles were noted, and one tile was missing altogether. Beneath the missing tile wasthe steel mounting plate for the L-band antenna, perhaps preventing a burn-through of the sort that would ultimately doom Columbia in 2003. STS-27 Atlantis is the most damaged launch-entry vehicle to return to Earth successfully.

A review team investigated the cause beginning with a detailed inspection of the Atlantis TPS damage, and a review of related inspection reports to establish an in-depth anomaly definition. An exhaustive data review followed to develop a fault tree and several failure scenarios. T

The Soviet Union produced a Space Shuttle of their own, the Buran. The name means heavy snowstorm. This unit, unlike the American shuttle, could be flown unmanned. It completed its first flight in 1988 in this manner, using the Energia launch vehicle. It unfortunately never made another flight, due to turmoil which resulted in the breakup of the former Soviet Union of countries. It was stored for possible further use at the launch site, now in the former Soviet republic of Kazakhstan.

It was destroyed in 2002, when the hanger it was stored in collapsed due to excessive snow load. The collapse also killed eight workers.

## Space flight can be fatal

There have been 18 astronauts/cosmonauts fatalities in-flight to this date, and more killed and injured in training. Space flight is, by its nature, a hazardous profession. Anything can go wrong. Astronaut Theodore Freeman was killed on final approach to Ellington AFB in Texas due to a goose strike on his aircraft. All the causes do not have to be high-tech.

The Soviet Vostok spacecraft accomplished the first human spaceflight. A total of 8 flights were made, 6 of them manned. It was a single passenger craft. The craft was designed such that if the retrorocket failed, the orbit would decay within about 10 days, and the cosmonaut had enough consumables to last that long. This scenario never happened.

Vostok-1 was launched in 1961. The mission was susccessful, right up to where the service module was to be jettisoned from the crew compartment. Cosmonaut Gagarin parachuted from the capsule at seven kilometers, and landed uninjured. The capsule laned by its own parachute, some 280 kilometers west of the intended point, causing a delay in recovery. Gagarin was found by a farmer and his family. He was given access to a telephone to call Moscow.

As on Vostok-1, the Vostok-2 service module failed to detach from the reentry module when commanded and reentry began with the former still attached. The conjoined modules gyrated violently until aerodynamic heating burned through the straps holding them together. Cosmonaut Titov ejected from the capsule as planned and parachuted separately to land safely.

Voskhod 1, in 1964, was the first spacecraft with a three-man crew in a modified Vostok capsule, It was also the first space flight during which cosmonauts performed in a shirt-sleeve-environment. However, flying without spacesuits was not done due to safety improvements in the Soviet spacecraft's environmental systems; but because the craft's limited cabin space did not have enough room. There was no provision for crew escape in the event of a launch or landing emergency for Voskhod.

The flight of Voskhod 2 lasted for 26 hours and 16 orbits. A manually controlled reentry was performed because of a malfunction of the automatic orientation devices for the retrofire, and the spacecraft landed in a pine forest far north of the target area. After locating the spacecraft, it took rescue crews a day to cut through the forest and bring the crew out on skis.

The Voskhod 2 mission had design modifications included the addition of an inflatable airlock to allow for extravehicular activity, while keeping the cabin pressurized so that the capsule's electronics wouldn't overheat. Cosmonaut Leonov performed the first-ever EVA as part of the mission. A fatality was narrowly avoided when Leonov's spacesuit expanded in the vacuum of space, preventing him from re-entering the airlock. In order to overcome this, he partially depressurized his suit to a potentially dangerous level. He succeeded in safely re-entering the ship, but he and fellow cosmonaut Belyayev faced further challenges when the spacecraft atmospheric controls flooded the cabin with 45% pure oxygen, which had to be vented to acceptable levels before re-entry .

## Soyuz

The Soyuz spacecraft superseded the Vostok and Voskhod manned craft by the late 1960's, using lessons learned from the previous programs.

The Soyuz-1 flight in 1967 was plagued with technical issues, and Cosmonaut Colonel Vladimir Komarov was killed when the descent module crashed into the ground due to a parachute failure. This was the first in-flight fatality in the history of spaceflight.

Prior to launch, Soyuz 1 engineers are said to have reported over 200 design faults to party leaders, but their concerns "were overruled by political pressures for a series of space feats to mark the anniversary of Lenin's birthday."

Problems began shortly after launch when one solar panel failed to unfold, leading to a shortage of power for the spacecraft's systems. Further problems with the orientation detectors complicated maneuvering the craft. By orbit 13, the automatic stabilization system was completely dead, and the manual system was only partially effective.

After 18 orbits, Soyuz 1 fired its retrorockets and reentered the Earth's atmosphere. Despite the technical difficulties up to that point, Komarov might still have landed safely. To slow the descent, the drogue parachute was deployed, followed by the main parachute. However, due to a defect, the main parachute did not unfold; the exact reason for the main parachute malfunction is disputed.

Komarov then activated the manually deployed reserve chute, but it became tangled with the drogue chute, which did not release as intended. As a result, the Soyuz reentry module hit the ground at about 90 mph.

A rescue helicopter spotted the descent module lying on its side with the parachute spread across the ground. The retrorockets were then seen to ignite, which concerned the rescuers since they were supposed to activate a few moments prior to touchdown. By the time the rescue team landed and approached, the descent module was in flames with black smoke filling the air and streams of molten metal dripping from the exterior. This is not good. The entire base of the capsule was burned through. By this point, it was obvious that Komarov had not survived,

A crew of three were killed on Soyuz 11, when the cabin depressurized prematurely just before reentry. Soyuz is widely considered the world's safest, most cost-effective human spaceflight vehicle, established by its unparalleled length of operational history. The latest versions are used to ferry Astronauts and Cosmonauts to the International Space Station.

There is a memorial monument at the site in the form of a black column with a bust of Komarov at the top, in a small park near the landing site. Komarov is commemorated in two memorials left on the Lunar surface: one left at Tranquility Base by Apollo 11, and the Fallen Astronaut plaque left by Apollo 15.

Soyuz 7 was part of a joint mission with Soyuz 6 and Soyuz 8 that saw three Soyuz spacecraft in orbit together at the same time, carrying a total of seven cosmonauts.

Soyuz 7 was to dock with Soyuz 8 and transfer crew, as the Soyuz 4 and Soyuz 5 missions had done. Soyuz 6 was to film the operation.

However, this objective was not achieved due to equipment failures. The Soyuz 8 crew were both veterans of the previous successful docking mission. This was the last time that the Soviet manned Moon landing hardware was tested in orbit, and the failure seems to have marked the death knell of that program.

Soyuz 11 was the only manned mission to board the world's first space station, Salyut 1. Soyuz 10 had soft-docked but had not been able to enter due to latching problems. The mission arrived at the space station on the 7th and departed on the 30th of June 1971. Soyuz 11's touchdown was wholly automatic, from the parachute deployment to the firing of solid-fueled soft-landing rockets in the base of the descent module. The mission ended in disaster, however, when the crew capsule depressurized during preparations for reentry, killing the three-man crew. The three crew members of Soyuz 11 are the only humans to have died outside the Earth's atmosphere.

"Outwardly, there was no damage whatsoever," On opening the hatch, the rescue ground crews found all three men in their couches, motionless, with dark-blue patches on their faces and trails of blood from their noses and ears. The apparent cause of death was suffocation. The crew did not have space suits.

A Soyuz capsule was testing the launch abort system in 1983, when a fuel spill from the launch vehicle caused the entire vehicle to be engulfed in flames. The vehicle on the pad exploded 2 seconds after the capsule escaped to safety. The escape system worked the way it was supposed to.

The Mir Space Station had a fire in the solid fuel oxygen generator onboard in 1997, as an American astronaut joined the Russian Cosmonauts in orbit. The location of the fire cut off one of the escape routes to a Soyuz capsule. The fire was successfully extinguished, but clearing the smoke took quite a while. The cause was found to be a piece of latex from a glove contaminating the Lithium Perchlorate canister during ground assembly. The material burns at over 750 degrees, and releases oxygen in the process. This time, it went very wrong. It was described by the Cosmonaut who had activated the cylinder as a "small, tiny baby volcano."An onboard volcano with three foot flames and molten metal. If the shell of the space station were beached, the fire would be extinguished in the vacuum of space, but by that time the entire crew of six would be dead. Due to access problems, only one of the crew could fight the fire at a time, but three fire extinguishers did the trick. Lessons learned from this incident lead to better procedures for Mir, and later, the International Space Station.

My good friend from high school, Astronaut Jay Apt, had a puncture in his glove during an Extra-Vehicular Activity (EVA) in 1991. The puncture was small, and his hand covered it. He was not aware of the hole until he came back inside the Shuttle, and took the glove off.

It's even dangerous if you're not going up in the rocket. In an incident in 1964, the third stage of a Delta rocket being prepared for launch ignited on the pad. There were two deaths and 8 injuries. What I recall from my Kennedy Space Center pad safety training is, just about anything there can kill you, and with toxic chemicals, if you can smell it, you're already dead.

## Soyuz TMA-1 flight computer problem

The new guidance computer for the Russian Soyuz TMA-1 caused an off-course landing in its first use in 2003. This was a concern for the crew of the International Space Station, as the Soyuz TMA-2 was docked to the station as the crew return vehicle, and it had the same computer. The Soyuz is normally controlled to skim the atmosphere to reduce its velocity, using a deceleration of 5g's. The center of gravity of the craft is off center by design, and by rolling the capsule, the tilt, and thus the lift, can be controlled. As in the Apollo days, too steep, you burn up, and too shallow, you skip off the atmosphere and head back to space.

The TMS-1 autopilot lost its references, and switched to backup. This simplier mode used a roll maneuver to even out the path, while resulting in a deceleration twice that of the nominal mode, and a very short landing footprint, compared to the nominal. In this case, the crew returned safely, and were spotted by a rescue team within two hours.

Initially, the Soyuz error was attributed to the American crewman pushing the backup mode activation button, but this was refuted by the crew, A software cause was sought. Software problems of potentially fatal effect had happened in 1988 (with the crew catching the error in time), and again in 1997, where two potentially catastrophic flaws were identified and mitigated by human intervention. One of these would have fired the reentry rockets in the wrong direction. The software was corrected. The Soyuz remains the main delivery and return vehicle for the  crew of the International Space Station.

Soyuz TMA-11 was a human spaceflight mission in 2007 using a Soyuz-TMA spacecraft to transport personnel to and from the International Space Station (ISS). The spacecraft was launched from the Baikonur Cosmodrome by a Soyuz FG launch vehicle.  TMA-11 remained at the station as an escape craft, and returned safely to Earth on April 19, 2008, after it had been replaced by Soyuz TMA-12. Although the vehicle landed safely, it suffered a partial separation failure which caused a ballistic re-entry that in turn caused it to land 475km from the intended landing point.

This was the second such event in a row for Soyuz TMA. Although the crew were recovered with no serious injuries, the spacecraft's hatch and antenna suffered burn damage during the unusual reentry. Yi So-Yeon, a Korean astronaut, was hospitalized after her return to South Korea due to injuries caused by the rough return voyage in the Soyuz TMA-11 spacecraft.

The principal reason for the unusual re-entry was said failure of the service module to separate normally as a result of one of five pyro-bolts malfunctioning. A similar anomaly occurred during the re-entry of Soyuz 5 in 1969.

It could have been worse. In 1965, the crew of the Voskhod-2, which had accomplished the first spacewalk, the capsule landed some 386 kilometers off course, and the crew had to spend the night in their capsule, due to the presence of bears and wolves in the area. Welcome back to Earth, tasty morsels.

# Lunar Fallen Astronaut Memorial

The Fallen Astronaut memorial is an aluminum sculpture created by Paul Van Hoeydonck. It is a small stylized figure, meant to depict an space traveler in a spacesuit, intended to commemorate the astronauts and cosmonauts who have died in the advancement of space exploration. It was commissioned and placed on the Moon by the crew of Apollo 15 at Hadley Rille on August 1, 1971, next to a plaque listing the fourteen men known at the time to have died. These are:

- Theodore C. Freeman (October 31, 1964, T-38 accident, first fatality in the astronaut corps )

- Charles A. Bassett II (February 28, 1966, aircraft accident during astronaut training)

- Elliot M. See Jr. (February 28, 1966, aircraft training accident)

- Virgil I. Grissom (January 27, 1967, Apollo 1 fire)

- Roger B. Chaffee (January 27, 1967, Apollo 1 fire)

- Edward H. White II (January 27, 1967, Apollo 1 fire)

- Vladimir M. Komarov (April 24, 1967, Soyuz 1 re-entry parachute failure)

- Edward G. Givens Jr. (June 6, 1967 killed in automobile accident before being assigned to a flight)

- Clifton C. Williams Jr. (October 5, 1967, mechanical failure in a NASA T-38 jet trainer, )

- Yuri A. Gagarin (March 27, 1968, killed in routine aircraft training flight)

- Pavel I. Belyayev (January 10, 1970, disease)

- Georgiy T. Dobrovolsky (June 30, 1971, Soyuz 11 re-entry pressurization failure)

- Viktor I. Patsayev (June 30, 1971, Soyuz 11 re-entry pressurization failure)

- Vladislav N. Volkov (June 30, 1971, Soyuz 11 re-entry pressurization failure)

## *ISS and its resupply*

The first part of the International Space Station went into orbit in 1998. It has been expanded since then, to such an extent that it is visible to the naked eye. Most of the construction and "heavy lifting" was done by the United States and Russia, with support from the European and Japanese Space Agencies. The ISS is actually the ninth inhabited Space Station in Earth Orbit, with previous Russian (USSR) and U. S. efforts. It has been continuously occupied, as of this writing, for more than 15 years. It has rotating crews from the United States and Russia, with other member countries supplying personnel, and paying customers – space tourists. It is periodically reboosted to higher altitudes, as its orbit decays due to atmospheric drag.

It has been necessary to occasionally conduct Debris Avoidance Maneuvers, to avoid know space debris nearing the station. It has been hit many times, but the hull has not been breached.

Although numerous failures and problems have affected Station operations and schedule, no one has been hurt of killed, and it has never been evacuated.

The Station has been crewed continuously since 2000. There are periodic resupply and logistics flights, carrying repair parts, new experiments, clean underwear, food oxygen, and water. Return flight carry trash, and burn up in the atmosphere. Some small payloads can be returned with the returning crew.

The Space shuttle was the primary supply "truck" for the Station, both during its construction and for part of its operational period. The Shuttle fleet was retired in 2011.

The Soyuz capsule is used to take crews up and back, but has limited cargo space. The Russian *Progress 62* vehicle is used for upgoing cargo It has a capacity of 2.8 tons.

Some of these flight have had problems M-12 failed to reach orbit, 2011. Around 325 seconds into the flight, the third stage of the Russian Soyuz-U rocket prematurely shut down, leaving Progress M-12M stranded on a sub-orbital trajectory. The failure, the first ever for a Progress since its introduction in 1978, could not have come at a worse time for the ISS, with the Space Shuttle recently retired, and commercial resupply flights not yet online.

The Progress 59 mission experienced serious problems shortly after its launch on April 28, 2015, and never attempted to dock with the station. Then, SpaceX's seventh cargo run failed less than three minutes after launch on June 28, when the Falcon 9 broke apart, apparently because of a faulty steel strut in the rocket's upper stage.

Commercial Programs

There has been an interest on NASA's part in making support of the International Space Station a commercial venture. To date, two American Aerospace Companies are involved. These are Orbital-ATK and SpaceX.

More companies are getting involved, since the business case for these flights has been established.

These all employ unmanned vehicles with several tons of cargo capacity, that dock autonomously with the Space Station.

<u>US SpaceX Dragon</u>

In 2012, Dragon became the first commercial spacecraft to deliver cargo to the International Space Station. SpaceX delivered cargo to the ISS in March 2013 and again in April 2014. The Dragon vehicle is designed to return to the surface, as opposed to the other units, which burn upon reentry. The Space-X capsule is recovered at sea. In February of 2015, the Dragon capsule returned 3,700 pounds to Earth from the station.

In June of 2015, a SpaceX resupply mission to the ISS failed when CRS-7 failed to reach orbit. This was attributed to a booster problem. Mission CRS-7 was also a failure. The Company Press Release said, "Preliminary analysis suggests the overpressure event in the upper stage liquid oxygen tank was initiated by a flawed piece of support hardware (a "strut") inside the second stage. Several hundred struts fly on every Falcon 9 vehicle, with a cumulative flight history of several thousand. The strut that we believe failed was designed and material certified to handle 10,000 lbs of force, but failed at 2,000 lbs, a five-fold difference."

In order to reduce launch costs, Elon Musk's private space company SpaceX is making a reusable booster from its existing Falcon-9 launch vehicle. The unit will have enough propellant to land vertically in a selected location, after delivering its payload to orbit. This will allow for refurbishment and reuse of the booster.

The first several flights were landed in the ocean, to show proof. of concept. The first flight suffered excessive roll rates during descent. The fuel was flung to the outside walls of the tank due to centrifugal forces, and the engines flamed out. Some debris was recovered. The second test achieved a soft landing, but the vehicle was not recovered due to rough seas. The third and fourth flights achieved zero velocity at zero altitude, but the boosters fell into the ocean (as planned). The next flight was scheduled to land on a floating recovery ship. Rough seas in the recovery area, with waves up to 3 stories,  were a major problem. Adding to that, one of the thrusters that kept the barge in position failed. The launch vehicle landed in the ocean.

The next attempt resulted in a hard landing on the target barge, and the vehicle fell overboard, and sank. One the next attempt, there was another hard but successful landing, that damaged some of the barge's deck equipment. The seventh landing attempt was also hard, with a stuck valve, and the stage tipped over on the barge, and burned.

An attempt to land the returning booster on dry land was accomplished successfully in December of 2015. More tests will be conducted.

The Falcon booster costs $60 million, and the cost to orbit will be vastly reduced with reuse of the expensive hardware.

The Orbital STK Cygnus vehicle uses Orbitals' Antares launch vehicle, and has a capacity of 7,000 pounds. It has suffered 3 failures in 4 launch attempts. In October  2014, the launch vehicle exploded just after leaving the launch pad

## *How to drown in Space*

On July 16, 2013, NASA cut short a spacewalk outside of the International Space Station after Italian astronaut Luca Parmitano reported water inside of his space suit helmet.

He felt  that somethingwas wrong. He said, "The unexpected sensation of water at the back of my neck surprises me — and I'm in a place where I'd rather not be surprised. I move my head from side to side, confirming my first impression, and with superhuman effort I force myself to inform Houston of what I can feel, knowing that it could signal the end of this EVA."

The engineers in Houston were made aware of the problem, and canceled the space walk.  The astronauts were told to make their way to the airlock, where they would reenter the space station. This was a good call, because Parmitano's situation was getting more dire by the minute:

He said, "As I move back along my route towards the airlock, I become more and more certain that the water is increasing. I feel it covering the sponge on my earphones and I wonder whether I'll lose audio contact. The water has also almost completely covered the front of my visor, sticking to it and obscuring my vision.... the water covers my nose – a really awful sensation that I make worse by my vain attempts to move the water by shaking my head. By now, the upper part of the helmet is full of water and I can't even be sure that the next time I breathe I will fill my lungs with air and not liquid."

He devised a plan of what to do if the water filled his helmet and covered his mouth: "The only idea I can think of is to open the safety valve by my left ear: if I create controlled depressurization, I should manage to let out some of the water, at least until it freezes through sublimation, which would stop the flow. But making a 'hole' in my spacesuit really would be a last resort." Yes, it is rarely advisable to punch a hole in your life support..

The two EVA astronauts made it back to the airlock, and into the station successfully.

Luca went on to say, "Now that we are repressurizing, I know that if the water does overwhelm me I can always open the helmet. I'll probably lose consciousness, but in any case that would be better than drowning inside the helmet."

The leak in Parmitano's suit seems to have been coolant water that leaked into his ventilation system through a faulty connector between the helmet and space suit.

### Let's get covered by Ammonia

On the STS-98 mission, on February 10, 2001, the Atlantis' astronauts went to work  preparing to install the 16-ton Destiny Laboratory on the International Space Station (ISS).

Astronauts Bob Curbeam and Tom Jones began preparing for a six-hour space walk to  install and hookup Destiny to the Unity module of the ISS. While Curbeam and Jones completed their spacewalk preparations, the Atlantis' robot arm was used to move an unoccupied Station docking port from Unity to a temporary parking location on the Station's external truss assembly. This cleared the way for Destiny's installation at the same berthing port on Unity.

Once the Astronauts were outside, they moved to two different locations with Curbeam disconnecting umbilical cables holding Destiny in Atlantis' cargo bay, and removing protective launch covers from Destiny's berthing mechanism. Jones climbed more than 40 feet up the exterior of the ISS where he acted as a visual guide for Ivins (operating the arm from inside the shuttle) as she slowly raised Destiny from Atlantis' payload bay.

With Destiny securely in place, Curbeam and Jones began connecting electrical, data and cooling lines between Destiny and rest of the Station. After completing their work outside, Curbeam and Jones would returned to Atlantis' airlock. So far, so good.

High above the bay, Ivins deftly flipped the 16-ton lab 180 degrees, moving it into position to attach to the station berthing port. When the lab was latched into position on the station,  a set of automatic bolts tightened to hold it permanently in place.  With the Destiny module secured to the station, Jones and Curbeam began connecting electrical, data, and cooling lines. While Curbeam was attaching a cooling line, a small amount of frozen ammonia crystals leaked,. but the leak was quickly stopped. The ammonia dissipated and vaporized, and it posed no problems as the crew continued their work. Because of the leak, however, flight controllers followed a decontamination procedure, ensuring no ammonia would enter Atlantis' cabin. All of the frozen ammonia had to be removed from the outside of the suit, or it would get into the airlock, and into the Shuttle cabin. Curbeam remained in the sun a half-hour to sublimate any ammonia crystals on his spacesuit while Jones brushed off the suit and equipment.

The spacewalkers performed a partial pressurization and venting of the shuttle airlock to flush out any ammonia before a final repressurization. Then, as the airlock began exchanging air with the shuttle cabin, Commander Ken Cockrell, Pilot Mark Polansky and Ivins wore oxygen masks in the cabin for about 20 minutes as a protective measure, allowing any residual ammonia to be cleansed from the cabin by shuttle life support systems. In the end, the crew reported no contamination or smell of ammonia in the cabin.The decontamination procedures lengthened the spacewalk to a final duration of seven hours, 34 minutes, more than an hour longer than originally planned.

# Satellite Payloads

Even if the payload survives the trip to orbit on the launch vehicle, it can still have problems. We'll explore several case studies here. If it is hard to get to orbit, it is very hard to get to another planet, and increasingly difficult to land there.

## *Mars Climate Orbiter*

The spacecraft was lost on Mars in September 1999. The requirements did not specify units, so JPL used SI (metric) units and the contractor Lockheed Martin used English units. This was not caught in the review process, and led to the loss of the $125 million mission. The spacecraft crashed due to a navigation error.

The computer architecture is a single RAD6000 cpu, with 128 megabytes of ram, and 18 megabytes of flash memory.

VxWorks, from Wind River systems, was the operating system with flight software developed at Lockheed Martin Corporation.

Sensors and Actuators included dual 3-axis gyros, a star tracker, dual sun sensors, eight thrusters, and four reaction wheels. An interesting error source in using 3 axis gyros (or other 3-axis devices such as magnetic torquer bars) is the naming of the axis. Every one has to agree on the names of the axes. Roll, pitch, yaw, x, y, z...all the data bases have to be consistent, and we all have to be on the same page. This error is usually caught in testing. Oh, and not relevant to Mars, as it has no real magnetic pole, but you did know the Earth's magnetic pole is at the geographic south pole, right?

The primary cause of this discrepancy was human error. Specifically, the flight system software on the Mars Climate Orbiter was written to calculate thruster performance using the metric unit Newtons (N), while the ground crew was entering course correction and thruster data using the Imperial measure Pound-force (lbf). This error has since been known as the *metric mix-up* and has been carefully avoided in all missions since by NASA.

"The root cause of the loss of the spacecraft was the failed translation of English units into metric units in a segment of ground-based, navigation-related mission software, as NASA has previously announced," said Arthur Stephenson, chairman of the Mars Climate Orbiter Mission Failure Investigation Board. "The failure review board has identified other significant factors that allowed this error to be born, and then let it linger and propagate to the point where it resulted in a major error in our understanding of the spacecraft's path as it approached Mars."

Reference

http://mars.jpl.nasa.gov/msp98/orbiter/

## Mars Rover Pathfinder

The computer in the Mars Rover Pathfinder suffered a series of resets while on the Martian surface.

The cpu Architecture was a single RS-6000 cpu, with 1553 and VMEbuses. The Software was the VxWorks operating system, with application code in c.

Sensors and Actuators included Sun sensors, a star tracker, a radar altimeter, accelerometers, and the wheel drive.

The Root Cause was Priority Inversion in the operating system. Pre-emptive priority thread scheduling was used. The watchdog timer caught the failure of a task to run to completion, and caused the reset. This was a sequence of tasks not exercised during testing. The problem was debugged from Earth, and a correction uploaded.

The failure was identified by the spacecraft as a failure of one task to complete its execution before the other task started. The reaction to this by the spacecraft was to reset the computer. This reset reinitializes all of the hardware and software. It also terminates the execution of the current ground commanded activities.

The failure turned out to be a case of priority inversion (how this was discovered and corrected is a fascinating story – see refs.) The higher priority task was blocked by the much lower priority task that was holding a shared resource. The lower priority task had acquired this resource and then been preempted by several of the medium priority tasks. When the higher priority task was activated, to setup the transactions for the next databus cycle, it detected that the lower priority task had not completed its execution. The resource that caused this problem was a mutual exclusion semaphore used to control access to the list of file descriptors that the select() mechanism was to wait on.

The Select mechanism creates a mutex to protect the "wait list" of file descriptors for those devices which support select. The vxWorks pipe() mechanism is such a device and the IPC mechanism used is based on using pipes. The lower priority task had called Select, which had called other tasks, which were in the process of giving the mutex semaphore. The lower priority task was preempted and the operation was not completed. Several medium priority tasks ran until the higher priority task was activated. The low priority task attempted to send the newest high priority data via the IPC mechanism which called a write routine. The write routine blocked, taking control of the mutex semaphore. More of the medium priority tasks ran, still not allowing the high priority task to run, until the low priority task was awakened. At that point, the scheduling task determined that the low priority task had not completed its cycle (a hard deadline in the system) and declared the error that initiated the reset.

References

http://www.nasa.gov/mission_pages/mars-pathfinder/

http://research.microsoft.com/en-us/um/people/mbj/Mars_Pathfinder/

## Phobos-Grunt

In November of 2010, the Russian Space Agency launched an ambitious mission to set a probe down on the small Martian moon Phobos, collect samples, and return them to Earth.

There was a failure of the spacecraft propulsion system that stranded the mission in Earth orbit. It re-enterred the Earth's atmosphere in January 2011.

Various causes were postulated for the failure, including interference by U.S. Radar, cosmic ray induced upsets, programming errors, and counterfeit chips.

The final report from Roscosmos cited software errors, failure of chips in the electronics, possibly due to radiation damage, and the use of non-flight qualified electronics, with inadequate ground testing.

Evidently, identical chips in two assemblies failed nearly simultaneously, so quickly that an error message was not generated. It was possible that the error was recoverable, as the spacecraft entered a safe mode with a proper sun orientation for maximum power. However, the design precluded the reset mode before the spacecraft left its parking orbit. This was major design oversight.

The identified chips that failed were 512k SRAM (static random access memory. The part numbers from the Russian report were checked by NASA's Jet Propulsion Lab, and were found to be among the most radiation susceptible chips they had ever seen. Bad choice. The chips could last in space a few days, and were barely acceptable for non-critical applications, The probably failure cause was single event latch-up, which is sometimes recoverable. In single event latch up, there is a single particle strike that latches up a transistor, preventing it from operating. Usually, if you turn it off and back on again, it will work. A lot of radiation damage to the underlying semiconductor lattice fixes itself after a while, a process called "annealing."

References

54

Klotz, Irene "Programming Error Doomed Russian Mars Probe," Discovery News, Feb. 7, 2012, news.discovery.com

de Carbonnel, Alissa "Russia races to salvage stranded Mars probe, " Reuters, 2011. www.reuters.com

Amos, Jonathan "Phobos-Grunt mars Probe loses its way just after launch," 9 Nov. 2011, BBC News, www.bbc.co.uk

Oberg, James "Did Bad memory chips Down Russia's Mars Probe?," Feb 2012, IEEE Spectrum, IEEE.org.

Friedman, Louis D. "Phobos-Grunt Failure Report Released," 2/6/2012, www.planetary.org/blogs/guest-blogs/lou-friedman

Phobos fail: What really happened to Russia's Mars Probe, Jan 19, 2012, RT.com.

## *Failure of Galaxy IV*

In 1998, the on-orbit Galaxy IV satellite's main control computer failed due to tin whiskers. This is a phenomena where, with the use of predominately tin solder, small conductive tendrils grow due to compressive stress, and cause electrical shorts. This occurs in several other metals as well. This phenomena was noted back in the vacuum tube era. It can be mitigated by adding lead to the solder, a practice that is now banned.

Tin whisker problems have been noted in heart pacemakers, and a false alarm at the Millstone Nuclear Plant in 2005

## *Spacecraft are not Waterproof*

A friend of the author was the fire chief at the nearest station to NASA Goddard Space Flight Center. For a while there had been a series of false fire alarms coming from the recently constructed Building 7-15 complex, containing, at the time, the largest thermal vacuum chamber in the world. The fire crews dutifully showed up for each alarm, and made sure it was really a false alarm before leaving.

One time, they entered the building when it was filled with smoke, toxic fumes, and … FIRE. Well, they did what they were trained to do, put water on it until it was suppressed.

Unfortunately, spacecraft are not designed to be water proof. For many years, the incident stood as the most expensive fire in U. S. history.

## Satellite on-orbit collision

A collision between two satellites occurred in February of 2009. One was a Russian Strela-class military satellite, massing 950 kilograms. The other was the commercial Iridium 33 communications satellite. What was the cause? They were in the same place at the same time. The Russian spacecraft had been deactivated, and was classified as space debris. The Iridium was operational, and was destroyed.

And, the bad news is, the collision created a thousand pieces of space debris larger than 4 inches, and many more smaller ones. In March 2012, a piece of the KOSMOS 2251 passed by the International Space Station, prompting the crew to take refuge in the attached Soyuz return craft as a precaution. The ISS frequently does obstacle avoidance maneuvers.

## Contour

The Comet Nucleus Tour spacecraft that launched in 2002, and failed shortly thereafter. It was to conduct a flyby of two or more comet nuclei, with an objective of high resolution imaging. Just after the ignition of the solid rocket for injection into solar orbit, the contact with the ground was lost. The actual cause is not known, but was postulated to be explosion of the boost motor, or structural failure of the spacecraft.

Ref: Bradley, Jr. Theron; Gay, Charles; Martin, Patrick; Stephenson, David; Tooley, Craig "Contour Comet Nucleus Tour Mishap Investigation Board Report," 2007.

ref:

discovery.nasa.gov/lib/presentations/pdf/**mishap_board_report**_503.pdf

# Transportation

"History repeats itself because no one was listening the first time."
Anonymous.

This section discusses failures in earthly modes of transportation, aircraft, highway, and rail. The (U. S.) National Transportation Safety Board (NTSB) keeps extensive databases of aviation events at:

http://www.ntsb.gov/investigations/reports_aviation.html

from their Mission Statement, on their website:

"The National Transportation Safety Board is an independent Federal agency charged by Congress with investigating every civil aviation accident the United States and significant accidents in other modes of transportation – railroad, highway, marine and pipeline. The NTSB determines the probable cause of the accidents and issues safety recommendations aimed at preventing future accidents."

I have not discussed the disappearance of Malaysia Airlines flight MH370 and some similar recent airline tragedies, because they have been analyzed widely in the press and on the Internet.

## Air France 447, and the Automation Paradox

Aircraft accidents get a lot of out attention. Air travel is safer than ever, but generates big headlines when something goes wrong. In June of 2009, Air France 447 left Rio de Janeiro heading to Paris. It was an Airbus A330. Unfortunately, it crashed into the Atlantic Ocean, killing all passengers and crew. The cause was completely unknown for quite a while, since the wreckage could not be located. Two years afterwards, the flight data recorders were located and retrieved from the ocean floor at 13,000 feet.

The official report on the accident said "that the aircraft crashed after temporary inconsistencies between the airspeed measurements, likely due to the aircraft's pitot tubes being obstructed by ice crystals, caused the autopilot to disconnect, after which the crew reacted incorrectly and ultimately led to an aerodynamic stall from which they did not recover. So we have two problems here. One, the pitot tubes clogged up, so airspeed could not be measured accurately, and the crew reacted inappropriately. There were 3 pitot tubes, and the problem with in-flight icing was known since the early days of aviation. Pitot tubes are heated to counter this problem. Why this triple redundancy did not work in this case is not known, although there does seem to be a common-cause error, which removed the redundancy.

The autopilot disengaged after a period of turbulence, and one of the flight deck crew took manual control. The engines auto-thrust control also disengaged, as designed. Evidently, at this time, the pitot tubes iced over, and an accurate measurement of airspeed was lost. In the mode the aircraft was in, stall warning was disengaged. Stall is when there is not enough airflow over the wings to generate lift, usually caused by low speed, or excessive angle of attack of the wind. The aircraft had a reported angle of attack of 35 degrees, way too much. The engines were operating a full power, with the aircraft nose angled up 35 degrees, upon impact with the ocean.

The aircraft had transmitted a series of automated messages , among them that there was a detected fault in the Air Data Inertial Reference Unit, that there was a disagreement among the three independent air data systems, and that there had been a fault in the flight management guidance system.

From the recovered recorders, it became clear that the pilots did not have a clear idea of the planes speed, due to inconsistent information. The final report mentioned, among other causes, that the flight crew "made inappropriate control inputs."

Part of the problem has been attributed to the Automation Paradox, where an automatic systems usually works so well without human input (such as the autopilot), the human operators are mostly kept out of the loop until something unexpected happens. Over-reliance on automated systems leads to complacency. At the same time, both the computer controls, and the pilots were without a valid speed indication.

References

http://www.bea.aero/docspa/2009/f-cp090601.en/pdf/f-cp090601.en.pdf

Jean-Pierre Otelli (2011). Erreurs de pilotage : Tome 5 (Pilot Error: Chapter 5). Altipresse. ISBN 979-10-90465-03-9.

Roger Rapoport (2011). The Rio/Paris Crash: Air France 447. Lexographic Press. ISBN 978-0-9847142-0-9.

Palmer, Bill (2013). Understanding Air France 447 (William Palmer. p. 218. ISBN 9780989785723.

## *Airbus A320-211 aircraft accident in Warsaw, Poland*

Quoted from the accident report:

"DLH 2904 flight from Frankfurt to Warsaw progressed normally until Warsaw Okecie TWR warned the crew that windshear exists on approach to RWY 11, as reported by DLH 5764, that had just landed. According to Flight Manual instructions PF used increased approach speed and with this speed touched down on RWY 11 in Okecie aerodrome. Very light touch of the runway surface with the landing gear and lack of compression of the left landing gear leg to the extent understood by the aircraft computer as the actual landing resulted in delayed deployment of spoilers and thrust reversers. Delay was about 9 seconds. Thus the braking commenced with delay and in condition of heavy rain and strong tailwind (storm front passed through aerodrome area at that time) aircraft did not stop on runway. In effect of the crash one crew member and one of the passengers lost their lives. The aircraft sustained damage caused by fire."

And, the problem does not need to be in the air. In September of 2004, The Los Angeles Air Route Traffic control Center lost radio communication with 400 aircraft, when the Center's voice comm system shut down unexpectedly. This was found to be due to a faulty software upgrade in the Voice Switching and Control System.

Reference

http://sunnyday.mit.edu/accidents/warsaw-report.html

## X-15

The X-15 Research Aircraft could fly to the boundary of Space in the 1950's, and became a training tool for Astronauts. They were carried to 45,000 feet under the wing of a B-52 aircraft, and dropped, after which their rocket engine would take them to 66 miles high. After the rocket engine burned all its fuel, the X-15 would return unpowered, and land on the dry lake beds at Edwards Air Force Base. After separation from the B-52, the flight took 10 minutes to reach altitude and land. Since it went above the atmosphere, the aircraft also included small maneuvering jets for control.

On the 191-st flight of an X-15, in November of 1967, something went terribly wrong for Air Force Major Mike Adams. The first problem was a large electrical arc from an exterior probe into the electrical system, after engine ignition. This evidently effected the flight control system. Less than a minute later, a second arc occurred. The aircraft became unresponsive to pilot inputs. At the peak of its climb, the aircraft was a a right angle to its flight path. This works OK if there's not much air. The pilot radioed to the ground the the aircraft "seems squirrely." As the aircraft descended into denser air, it went into a spin, but the aerodynamic and thruster controls were able to stop this. However, at this point the aircraft was in an inverted dive, with violent oscillations in all three axes. The aircraft broke apart at 63,000 feet.

Lessons learned from this unfortunate incident were used to improve the Apollo Lunar Lander flight control system. Major Adams was posthumously awarded Astronaut Wings.

Reference

NASA system Failure Case Study, march 2011, Vol. 5, Issue 3.

## Nuclear Weapons Mistake

Generally, this title heading is not good news. In August of 2007, a B-52 bomber was loaded with cruise missiles with inert warheads, and went from North Dakota to Louisiana. When they landed, it was discovered that they were live weapons, not inert. There were extensive safeguards and procedures in place to prevent this from happening. The handling crew in North Dakota evidently did not follow established procedures to ensure the warheads were actually inert. Despite a 5-step process, the error was not caught before flight. Besides their possible activation (there are extensive safeguards to prevent that, of course), the weapons were exposed to possible theft. The procedures were modified so that real and inert warheads are not stored in the same facility.

Reference

NASA, System Failure Case Studies, May 2011, Vol 5, Issue 5.

## Polish Tram take-over

In 2008, a bored 14-year old took over the Tram System in his hometown of Lodz, Poland. It was like having his own large scale model train that he could operate out his bedroom windows. Unfortunately, he managed to derail 4 vehicles, and injure twelve people. He was a good computer hacker, but not a good tram driver.

He spent hours on the tram system, and observed the signals and switches were controlled by the driver/operator, using an infrared device. He built his own device, a modified tv remote control. He kept careful notes in his school notebook about the track plan, switch locations, and control protocols.

He was charged by the police with endangering public safety. One could say this was a design failure in the control system that did not include adequate security. Who is driving the Tram you are on? (Here in the U.S. We would refer to this as an Urban light rail vehicle, running on its own tracks, not shared with a regular rail line. An example is the Baltimore, Maryland, light rail system.)

Reference

www.theregister.co.uk/2008/01/11/tram_hack

## NSW Rail Outage

In April of 2011, a signals problem on the New South Wales Railroad System (Australia) caused all signals to turn red. This was the safest approach, of course, but resulted in over 100,000 passengers to be stranded for several hours. There were 847 trains delayed, and 240 had to be canceled. No one was injured, but a lot of people were inconvenienced.

The Root Cause was found to be two failed electrolytic capacitors plus a software design problem in the Advanced Train Running Information Control System (ATRICS) system. The capacitors in the network interface hardware at the Sydenham signal box put the systems local area network into a partially failed state that the software couldn't handle. The architecture was a Gigabit optical LAN with switches and routers, protected from the Internet by a firewall. A switch failed due to the failure of two capacitors. Unfortunately, it was a partial failure, where the equipment kept switching between failed mode and operational mode. The rest of the system could not keep up with the reconfigurations. The system had to be turned off, the failed unit unplugged, and the system then turned back on (ie, reboot).

The system had previously operated correctly for 8 years. A root cause analysis was conducted. The incident pointed out a design weakness, that was addressed. An FMEA was suggested for the entire system.

Reference

Railcorp Signal and Control System, Engineering Technical Investigation, Sydenham Signal Box Failures on April 12th, 2011, 29 April 2011. NSW Transport RailCorp.

## DC Metro Red Line

In June of 2009, the Washington, D.C. Metro system suffered a train-on-train collision, resulting in eight deaths, and 80 injuries. This happened on the system's Red Line, near the Fort Totten station. Train 112 read-ended Train 214 at evening rush hour. This was the deadliest crash in Metro history. It was handled by Emergency Responders as a mass causality incident. It involved over 200 firefighters in a 3-alarm situation, and later, heavy moving and lifting equipment.

The first car of the moving train impacted and climbed over the stationary train. Some passengers had been ejected from the cars by the force of the collision.

The National Transportation Safety Board was involved. Well, all they had to do was hop on the Metro from their downtown office. Actually, they drove.

Several possible fault causes were postulated, including operator error, brake failure, and faults(s) in the computerized signals system. The centralized controller for the system can apply a train's brakes, but this system had failed in the past. The moving train did have its manual emergency brake activated by the operator, who died in the crash. At the time, the train was operating in automatic mode. It was also noted that the lead car, which housed the operator, was several month's overdue for scheduled maintenance on the brakes.

The NTSB report said, "The first car of the striking train overrode the rear car of the stationary train, and much of the survivable space ..was compromised." Do not sit in compromised spaces during a collision.

An important issue with 3rd-rail systems such as Metro is that the 600 volts (DC) in the $3^{rd}$ rail can certainly toast you. The third rail power will not necessarily be cut off immediately after an accident, and provides a hazard to evacuees, particularly in dark tunnels. It can also provide a hazard to first responders, but they are trained to assume the line is "Hot" until shown otherwise. There is also the possibility that a derailed car can contact the $3^{rd}$ rail, and itself become energized. None of this was an issue during the incident discussed.

Investigation showed that the detectors on the section of track that the stationary train occupied had failed to detect the presence of that train. So, as far as the automatic system was concerned, these was no reason to apply the brakes. Metro had replaced some 20,000 track circuit relays some ten years earlier, after they began to fail far shorter than their advertised 70-year life. It

63

turns out, that particular track circuit had failed some 18 months before the accident. During the investigation, an additional six were found to be malfunctioning. Service was interrupted on the line for a week.

The official NTSB report said the root cause was the faulty track circuit. The operator realized the system had malfunctioned, and applied the emergency brake, but too late to stop the train. The system was restricted to operating in manual mode.

I take the Metro system from the suburbs into the city on occasion, and now I ride in the middle cars, never the end ones. One convenience on the Metro, and a good safety factor, is that cell phone service is provided in the Metro tunnels.

In a follow-on incident In January of 2010, a Team of Safety Inspectors was nearly hit a a Metro Train. It was termed a "near-miss" situation, with the inspectors scrambling out of the path of the oncoming train, but no injuries were reported. The incident occurred near the Braddock Road Station in Alexandria, Virginia.

The primary cause was determined to be excessive speed of the train. The Operator erred in traveling too fast in a work zone. It was unclear whether the train operator was aware of the work zone. The work zone rules had been established after incidents in 2005-2006 in which four workers were struck by trains, and killed.

Another incident occurred in January of 2015, in which an electrical malfunction called a train to stall in a tunnel, and generated a large amount of smoke. There are ventilation fans in place for this scenario, but they seemed to be operated in the wrong direction, forcing smoke into the tunnel. Generally, you are safer in the train, where you can't come in contact with the 600 volt third-rail. About 250 commuters had to wait 30 minutes or so to be evacuated by emergency responders, with most having breathing difficulties, and there was one fatality.

Reference

www.washingtonpost.com

NASA System Failure Case Studies, August 2011, Vol 5, Issue 8.

## 17-Mile Grade train accident

The 17 mile grade is an east-west rail line in far Western Maryland, climbing Backbone Mountain. It was built by the Baltimore and Ohio Railroad in 1853, and was the largest challenge to American railroads until the Transcontinental line was built 20 years later. Heading west, it climbs from the Potomac River to Altamont, Maryland, the highest point, at 2,628 feet above sea level. The construction of the rail line enabled the railroad to reach the Ohio River, and connected freight traffic to the Port of Baltimore. After the construction of the grade, the U.S. Congress passed a bill restricting all rail lines in the United States to be built with a lesser grade than the 17-mile.

Today, the line is a key resource for coal and merchandise trains. The line is not only steep, but has numerous curves. As much as it is a challenge to climb, it is a test of train handling to descend with loads. Did I mention the near-Alaskan weather in that region during the winter? People who live there admit to two seasons, Winter, and July.

The curves and steepness was the cause of an accident with fatalities in January, 2000. A coal train descending eastward derailed 76 loads of coal, one loaded coal car crashing into a house, and killing 15 year old Eddie Rogers. It took 12 hours of digging to recover the body. The NTSB indicated that the probable cause of the January 2000 derailment was "the railroad's practice of including dynamic braking in determining maximum authorized speed without providing the engineer with real-time information in the status of the dynamic braking system." The train's speed from the event recorders (black boxes) was 55 miles per hour, in an area where the allowed speed is 25 miles per hour. Behind the engines were over 10,500 tons of cars and cargo.

There were actually 3 derailment incidents. At milepost 210.6, 17 cars derailed. At 209.8, 16 cars derailed. Finally, at 208.2, 41 cars derailed. The milepost numbers decrease going eastward. After demolishing the house, the coal cars went on to demolish a natural gas regulating station. Luckily, no explosion ensued.

Let's look at some definitions. Each car of the 80-car train would be carrying 100 tons of coal. Although each car and the locomotives have friction brakes, they would rapidly overheat and burn out trying to control the speed on the mountain. In steam engine days, there would have been a much shorter train, with less tonnage. Modern diesel locomotives use dynamic brakes, meaning the traction motors are run backwards and generate electricity that is dissipated as heat, slowing the train. The friction brakes, which involve metal brake shoes operating on steel wheels, can quickly generate enough heat to burn. Another problem encountered in this area is snow and ice build-up between the brake shoes and the wheel, minimizing brake function.

The latest derailment on the grade was in February, 2014, when 73 loaded coal cars derailed just west of the location of the Jan 2000 incident.

Reference

www.times-news.com (Cumberland, MD)

## *Montgomery Co. (MD) Traffic Light Problem*

The traffic signal system in Montgomery County, MD, outside Washington, D. C. erred in November 2009 when it did not enter "rush hour mode." This meant that rush hour optimizations for global traffic flow did not occur, inconveniencing 10's or 100's of thousands of commuters. The traffic lights were operating properly and safely, but the network of traffic lights was not being co-ordinated to optimize traffic flow across the county.

Also, but not related, a simultaneous software glitch in the Metro train system occurred that blocked usage of debit cards for fare payment. This provides yet more empirical evidence for the existence of Murphy's law. It was feared at the time that these incidents were a result of cyber-terrorism. The outages directly affected some of my students getting to my Embedded Computing class at the time. This lasted for four rush-hours.

The traffic light system relied on a 16-bit DataGeneral minicomputer, then 29 years old. The Software was custom. The systems had failed, and it was the source, via Lan, of the network time. Local clocks drifted, and the systems went out of synchronization (but, was always safe).

The root cause of the problem was that the central computer failed to distribute timing information over the network to the individual intersection controllers. The computer was updated.

In another incident in July of 2010, the fire alarm went off in the Montgomery County traffic signal computer room. The power automatically shut off, and water was accumulating under the raised floor. However, no fire was found. The water was not from fire fighting, but from a failure in the air conditioning's condensation pump. During the outage, traffic lights operated on local control, and no problems were seen. This was rapidly corrected, without the chaos of the previous incident.

Reference

www.wtop.com

http://nancyfloreen.blogspot.com/2010/07

## Ford Nucleon

In the 1950's, the promise of free and safe nuclear energy captured the imagination. We could harness this; we could control it. This was before the Three-Mile Island incident, before Chernobyl. In 1957, the Ford Motor Company considered a car powered by a small nuclear reactor. Using the same system as nuclear submarines, but smaller, the car would go about 5,000 miles, before the modular reactor needed to be swapped out. The reactor was in the rear of the car, some distance from the passengers. One could speculate on what would happen in a rear end collision. I don't think this would be a good candidate for the shade-tree mechanic. A working prototype was never produced, but a lot of design work was done.

## Toyota sudden acceleration issue

There was a problem observed when statistically significant numbers (4.51 per 100,000) of Toyota vehicle owners reported sudden unintended acceleration – the car would go faster on its own. These were attributed to driver error or floor mats, but no problem could be found. No other brand had the same problem. What kicked the investigation into high gear was a high profile 2009 crash of a California Highway Patrol officer and his family involving a 2009 Lexus.

The Prius model had been recalled for brake-related software issues, but Toyota adamantly denied any such problem with the engine control software. The problem was not reproducible. An intermittent like this is the worst case debugging scenario.

There were hundreds of lawsuits against Toyota, but no real hard evidence. The facts came to light in the pretrial investigations of the Bookout v Toyota wrongful death lawsuit. The problem had been investigated by Toyota computer engineers, the National Highway Traffic Safety Administration, NASA, and Mike Barr, of the Barr Group. The pieces finally clicked for Mike. (In full disclosure, Mike has been a repeat guest lecturer in my Embedded Computer systems class). In this particular case, a woman had been killed, and another seriously injured when a 2005 Toyota Camry overturned on an Oklahoma off-ramp. Toyota was found liable, and the injured driver was awarded $1.5 million, with another $1.5 million to the family of the dead woman in 2013.

Expert witnesses testified that after extensive software code review and testing, the electronic throttle control code was defective. The change of a single bit was shown by Barr to be able to trigger an inadvertent acceleration. Mike and his team of 7 produced a detailed 800 page report on the issue. NHTSA had closed the Toyota case in 2011, having found no problems. In support of NHTSA, NASA's Engineering and Safety Center examined the 280,000 lines of source code code, and found some problems, but not THE problem. Given more time, they probably would have, but they had a deadline for the report to be issued. Mike's expertise is in embedded computers with real-time operating systems, and he examined the Toyota code for more than a year.

An Embedded computer is a computer combined with various sensors and actuators in a system. The primary purpose of the embedded computer is the control the system functions. It is not general purpose. There is an embedded computer in your mobile phone, for example.

A real time operating system is an operating system that can meet deadlines. Windows, a desktop operating system, is NOT a real time operating system. (Although some companies have mis-used it like that and paid people like me to fix it.) An example of a real time operating system is VxWorks, from Wind River Systems. In terms of a real-time system, the right answer, late, is wrong and leads to failure.

Toyota had introduced its ETCS-i (Electronic Throttle Control System – Intelligent) in the 2002 Camry model, to replace the mechanical linkage between the accelerator pedal and the throttle valve in the engine. This was drive-by-wire. The position of the accelerator pedal was read by a sensor, and translated to a throttle motor control signal. (Car manufacturers are testing steer-by-wire systems, where there is no mechanical linkage between the steering wheel and the steering linkage at the tires. Aircraft had used fly-by wire systems for quite a while. In fact, very high performance aircraft are designed unstable (for performance reasons) and can't actually be flown by an unassisted human.)

There were unprotected critical variables in the code. The values in these memory-resident items were critical to the operation of the unit, but could be inadvertently overwritten by other code. Mike had locked-room access to the proprietary Toyota software under non-disclosure terms, and used a simulator to examine its behavior in detail. He found that certain task (software sub-programs with a specific function) could die (cease to run) without the safety feature "watchdog" responding appropriately. The watchdog is a small timer in hardware that, unless periodically reset by the software, will reset the computer. It is a protection against tasks that run too long, or enter an "infinite loop."They also found problems in worse case stack usage. The stack is a data structure in memory with a defined size. If a programs accidentally writes beyond the end of the stack, other memory entities are corrupted. Also Mike noted that the analysis that Toyota had given to NASA had "big mistakes."

Interestingly, cars now have a "blackbox" function somewhat like the ones in aircraft that record events. No indication of the sudden acceleration was ever found in the black box recordings, which seemed to point to another source other than the computer. However, it was found that the code that wrote the data to the "blackbox" memory was flawed as well. Ultimately, the incidents lead Toyota to a Billion dollar loss, and there are continuing lawsuits.

The information is now in the public domain. That Toyota, a highly respected manufacturer, could have made so many errors surprised many. But they are a car company, not a software company. A hard lesson to learn is that engineering best practices and quality control procedure apply to software as well.

In the software, with many branches and modes, there were "tens of millions of combinations; too many to test." The fail-safes were not adequate to their tasks. One shocking revelation is that NHTSA had no guidelines or standards for safety critical software. The Federal Airline Administration has these for aircraft, and the Food and Drug Administration has these for medical devices. You're on your own, with cars. On top of that, reliable software is costly. Maybe we can cut some corners here, and not get caught.

Also, in October of 2013, Toyota recalled some 800,000 cars due to...spiders. They like to build webs, and those tend to clog things up, and collect water. Three unintended air bag deployments were noted, and 35 cases of warning lights coming on. Don't spiders catch bugs?

References

*Technical Assessment of Toyota Electronic Throttle Control (ETC) Systems*, U. S. Department of Transportation, National Highway Traffic Safety Administration, February 2011.

*Technical Support to the National Highway Traffic Safety Administration (NHTSA) on the Reported Toyota Motor Corporation Unintended Acceleration (UA) Investigation,* NASA Engineering and Safety Center, Assessment TI-10-00618, January 18, 2011.

Barr, Michael, "Toyota's Embedded Software Image Problem," Barr Group, March 19, 2010.

Yoshida, Junko "Toyota Case: Single Bit Flip That Killed," EE Times, 10/25/13.

Psiropoulos, Dean "Computer overload threatens auto safety," WWW.embedded.com 2/4/10.

## USS Yorktown

"It is found that anything that can go wrong at sea generally does go wrong sooner or later, so it is not to be wondered that owners prefer the safe to the scientific..." Alfred Holt, 1877.

The US Navy Aegis Missile Cruiser Yorktown (CG-48) was dead in the water off Cape Charles, Virginia, in September of 1997. The Yorktown was the floating testbed for the Navy's Smart Ship Program, and that wasn't going well. All ships systems were shut down, and the ship had to be towed to port. The problem was a software error.

Now, I'm not a Naval Engineer, but I would think having a warship dead in the water with all systems shut down would be a bad thing. The Yorktown had a distinguished career before it was automated, including facing down the Soviet Fleet in the Black Sea as a part of Operation Freedom of Navigation.

The onboard computer resources included twenty-seven dual 200 MHz Pentium Pro-based desktop computers and a PentiumPro server on a fibre optic lan. The Software was Windows-NT 4.0 with custom application software. This was designed to reduce manpower needs by 10% and costs in operating the ship.

The computers held control over all of the ships systems, bridge, damage control, steering, engine control, weapons, and navigation. This included the radar, missiles, guns, damage control, and the 80,000 horsepower turbine engine None of which was working at the time.

The root cause was found in Software. A database error caused a critical error in engine room control, resulting in shutdown. It was an attempted division by zero, entered by mistake. (was this human error? Why no bounds checking?) There was a lack of redundancy, no error segmentation, and insufficient or non-existent back up systems

But, surely there have been lessons learned, and progress in this area. The Navy's new USS Zumwalt guided missile destroyer (DDG1000) is described as "a floating data center." It relies on off-the-shelf IBM blade servers running Red Hat Linux on multiple virtual machines, and multi-millions of lines of code. The ship's systems were integrated by Raytheon. The operations center of the ship is described as being more like the Starship Enterprise than any known surface warship. There is a shipboard internet for command and control traffic, as well as voice traffic. The operations center controls communication both within and external to the ship, the weapons systems, and the propulsion (this is beginning to sound familiar.) Surely, they learned from the Yorktown incident, didn't they?

References

Slabodkin, Gregory "Software glitches leave Navy Smart Ship dead in the water," GCN Government News, July 13, 1998.

Gallagher, Sean "The Navy's newest warship is powered by Linux," www.arstechnica.com, Oct. 18, 2013.

## Titanic

The RMS Titanic is a classic failure case study that has been extensively studied, in spite of the difficulties that the wreckage is 12,000 feet below sea level. The tragic incident captured the imagination of the World when it happened, and that interest has continued to the current day (Movie spoiler alert: the ship sinks).

Positive effects of the disaster included the mandate of enough lifeboats for all passenger and crew, and lifeboat training and drills. It also resulted in the mandating of radio watches on passenger ships 24x7, and in formation of the International Ice Patrol.

After striking the iceberg, the ship eventually broke in two and sank. The debris field on the sea floor spans an area of 3 by 5 miles. It is known that 5 of the watertight compartments were breached. The root cause of the disaster has not been determined, as it may involve a combination of factors. Metal fatigue in the cold waters, and the quality of the rivets have been cited. Workmanship was hopefully not a cause, as many of the workers from the shipyard in Belfast were chosen to go on the maiden voyage as a reward for their work.

Numerous books and articles have been written on the engineering details of the ship. A good place to start is: http://www.titanichistoricalsociety.org/

## World War -2 Liberty ships

The World War-2 Liberty ships were mass-produced to fill a need for transportation of war material to Europe. The construction time went from 230 days to a later average of 24 days, although one was completed in 4 ½ days. They were built in assembly line fashion in American shipyards from prefabricated parts. They were operated by the sailors of the Merchant Marine, not an armed service.

Of the more than 2,700 built, three were known to have broken in half and sunk, due to brittle fracture. This was shown not to be due to the relatively new fabrication method of welding versus riveting of plate, but due to the grade of steel used, in combination with the heavily loaded ships being operated in freezing Arctic waters. Many seamen lost their lives, not due to hostile action, operating the supply pipeline to Europe.

Reference:_Elphick, Peter *Liberty: The Ships That Won the War,* Naval Institute Press; 1st Edition, 2001, ISBN-1557505357.

# Infrastructure

"That men do not learn very much from the lessons of history is the most important of all the lessons that hisotry has to teach." Aldous Huxley.

In this section, we will discuss failures in infrastructure, due to engineering problems, or Nature's intervention.

## *Tacoma Narrows Bridge*

The Tacoma Narrows Bridge opened in 1940, to span Puget Sound in Washington State. It was soon found to have a strange behavior that got it the nickname, "Galloping Gurtie." The strong winds down the Sound caused aeroelastic flutter, which lead to complete failure of the bridge within a few months. This was captured on movie film. This phenomena was not well known before World War 2.

Reference

Billah, K.; R. Scanlan (1991). "Resonance, Tacoma Narrows Bridge Failure, and Undergraduate Physics Textbooks" (PDF). *American Journal of Physics* **59** (2): 118–124.

## Pipelines

Pipeline systems are routinely used to transport petroleum products and natural gas over large distances safely and efficiently, without use of rail or road infrastructure. On occasion, accidents will happen.

In 1999, a pipeline operated by Olympic Pipeline Company exploded near Bellingham, WA. The disaster started around 3:25 pm when the 16-inch diameter gasoline pipeline ruptured due to various errors and malfunctions. The gasoline vapors exploded at 5:00, sending a fireball down Whatcom Creek. Three people died in the accident. The pipeline was transporting gasoline from Cherry Point Refinery to terminals in Seattle and Portland, Oregon. A pressure relief valve that was not configured properly failed to open in the pipeline, which resulted in a surge of pressure after an automatic valve shut for reasons unknown. This resulted in the line rupturing.

When the nearby Bellingham Fire Department arrived, massive amounts of gasoline had entered the creek and the fumes were overwhelming. The fire department alerted Olympic Pipeline of the problem, and evacuated the area.

The gasoline vapor exploded at 5 pm, making Whatcom Creek a river of fire.. The black smoke from the explosion was visible in Vancouver, and extended upwards to 30,000 feet. Interstate 5 was closed, and the Coast Guard stopped maritime traffic in Bellingham Bay as a safety precaution.

Three people died in the accident. The first victim was fly fishing in the creek, when he fell unconscious due to the fumes, and drowned in the creek, luckily dying before the explosion. Unfortunately. two children, aged 10, were playing near the creek during the explosion. Both survived the blast, but died the next day in the hospital.

A lot of property damage was caused by the explosion. Buildings had blown-out windows, with one house totally destroyed. The water treatment plant of the city was destroyed. The rupture had allowed 277,000 US gallons of gasoline to escape into the creek bed.

After a three-year investigation, investigators pointed to a series of failures most of which were blamed on Olympic Pipeline. The company had failed to properly train employees, and had a faulty pressure relief valve. Olympic Pipeline faced a seven-count indictment after the investigation concluded in 2002. The companies pleaded guilty to several of the charges, leading to a $112 million settlement. This was the first conviction under the 1979 Hazardous Liquid Pipeline Safety Act.

Similar incidents have occurred in Europe, Africa, and India.

I'm not sure which section to put this in, so I'll put it here.. In 1989 near Ufa, Tartarstan, Russia, sparks from two passing trains on the Kuybyshev Railway caused gas leaking from an LPG pipeline to explode. Workers with the pipeline noticed pressure dropping in the line, so they increased pressure instead of searching for a leak. Trees up to 4 kilometers away were felled by the blast, and 2 locomotives and 38 passenger cars on the trains were derailed. Up to 645 people were reported killed. It was the deadliest railway accident in Russian and Soviet history. So, increasing the pressure solved the pressure drop problem. But, that wasn't THE problem.

References

www.youtube.com/watch?v=AJRwePrctGw

http://www.oig.dot.gov/library-item/3133

http://www.tripadvisor.com/Attraction_Review-g298521-d2578967-Reviews-Road_Museum_of_Kuybyshev_Railway_History-Samara_Samara_Oblast_Volga_District.html

## *Hurricane Sandy – lessons learned.*

Hurricane Sandy was a Superstorm that hit the east coast of the United States in 2012. It became the largest Atlantic hurricane on record. It claimed the lives of 286 people, and was responsible for over $68 billion dollars in damage. Mandatory evacuations occurred all along the east coast, including New Jersey and New York. Major damage to infrastructure was seen across the United States. It has such devastating effects, that the name "Sandy" was retired by the World Meteorological Organization.

In New York City, unaccustomed to having to deal with Tropical Storms, the damage was extensive. At that point, Sandy was a Category-1 storm (lowest level of severity). The subway system flooded, the sewer system overflowed 10 billion gallons of raw sewage, the electrical grid went down, and there was extensive water and wind damage in lower Manhattan. The storm resulted in power loss and deaths in Canada, and halted shipping on the Great Lakes.

The storm was documented rather completely because of the population density of the areas effected. Most importantly, there were a lot of lessons learned that may somewhat mitigate the effects of future storms of this magnitude in heavily populated areas.

There are many stories, and many lessons-learned from the incident. We'll touch on a few of these. Manhattan is the heart of American financial, with data and computation systems hosted in major data centers. Due diligence says those firms have an established Business Continuity Plan, and a Disaster Recovery Plan. But, what were the assumptions that those plans were written to? What is the backup-backup plan when the back-up plan fails? Who anticipated the severity of the Superstorm? That wasn't credible, was it?

As a backup, those data centers routinely have diesel generators for back up power in case of problems with th electrical grid. The assumption is that power will be restored within 24 hours. The fuel tanks were sized to hold 3 days worth of fuel. Many data centers were without electrical service for a week or more. Many could not get fuel deliveries, due to access issues. The damage to the cell infrastructure meant that many cell phones were not working. (as a side note, cell towers generally have a generator with 24 hours of fuel. After that period of time, some one has to refuel the generator.) Another problem in the data centers was loss of water for equipment cooling. On the other hand, with emergency generators located in the basements, many were flooded and could not operate. One facility had generators on an upper floor, and employees formed a bucket brigade to haul fuel cans up all those flights of stairs.

The damage caused by Sandy was exceeded only by Hurricane Katrina on the Gulf Coast in 2005. Category 5 Katrina was the costliest and most deadliest natural disaster in the United States. So far.

The major damage due to Katrina was because of the storm surge protection system failures. The storm surge was forecast to be at 28 feet, much higher than the levees were designed for. Eighty percent of the city was underwater. Most of the residents of New Orleans were evacuated from the city, some going as far as Houston, Texas. The name "Katrina" was retired from the Atlantic Hurricane naming list.

References

Hachman, Mark "How CoreSite survived Sandy," Nov 7, 2012,

http://slashdot.org/topic/datacenter

*Hurricane Sandy FEMA After-Action Report*, U.S. Department of Homeland Security , Federal Emergency Management Agency, CreateSpace Independent Publishing Platform, September 27, 2013, ISBN-1492831573.

# Medical

This section discusses hazards in Medical Devices and procedures that are intended to save us. Medical personnel and facilities have to deal with deadly viruses all the time. Now, they have to deal with viruses in their equipment and data systems as well.

Another cheery note from the U. S. Food and Drug administration is that recalls in faulty medical equipment are due to software problems in 24% of the cases. Like many other domains, the medical device field has been forced to focus on software process, software quality, and standards.

Medical devices also have to provide security and privacy, as well as safety, and sometimes these are conflicting requirements. Avoiding counterfeit software updates, malware, is as important. Remote programming of your heart pacemaker by sources unknown is not a good idea. Neither is interfering with a deep brain stimulation device.

Security vulnerabilities were discovered in an automated defibrillator. A website used to provide software updates to respirators was found to be infected with malicious code. Medical databases are frequent targets of attacks regarding identify theft.

Implantable medical devices such as pacemakers and insulin pumps can be remotely accessed, and thus require security. Who do you want controlling your drug dose, a medical professional or a bored teenage hacker in an Internet cafe in a 3$^{rd}$ world country?

A lot of standalone medical equipment in patient and treatment rooms is based on the Windows operating system and the pc architecture. Unfortunately, manufacturers can't allow frequent system updates because the Food & Drug Administration requires the entire device to be re-certified, which can be a multi-year process. You know all those updates you get almost daily when you power up your pc or laptop? Those aren't happening in the Medical world.

IEC 62304 has became the benchmark standard for the development of medical device software, whether standalone software or otherwise, in both the EU and the US.

The Food and Drug Administration keeps a database of interesting problem case studies. These are categorized as Adverse Effects, Product Use Error, Product Problem, and Problem with Different Manufacturer of Same Medicine. You can submit your own MedWatch voluntary Reporting Form online at https://www.accessdata.fda.gov/scripts/medwatch/ . They also keep a handy database of product recalls. Generally, you don't want to know what the Worst that can happen is. But, there is the "Extreme Weather Effects on Medical Devices" section for your further reading enjoyment.

In general, less than 1% of implanted medical devices fail. One chance in a hundred? Is that a good deal. Maybe, unless your defibrillator shorts out and kills you. That has been documented.

References

https://threatpost.com/en_us/blogs/fda-software-failures-responsible-24-all-medical-device-recalls-062012.

Talbot, David "Computer Viruses are 'Rampant' on Medical Devices in Hospitals,"MIT Technology Review, Oct. 17, 2012, www.technologyreview.com

http://www.accessdata.fda.gov/scripts/MedWatchLearn/health-professionals.htm

## Therac-25 ( THE Medical device failure study)

The classical failure of a medical treatment device was the Therac-25 . There were six known accidents involving radiation overdoses leading to death and serious injury.

The early machine was based on a 16-bit PDP-11 minicomputer, running custom software..There were 8 main routines. "Treat" was the main monitor task. It rescheduled itself after every subroutine. The housekeeper task took care of status interlocks and limit checks. The computer controlled the radiation gun positioning, and intensity control.

The Root Cause of the problems was shown to be overly complex programs written in unreliable styles, with a confusing user interface that caused user error,

References

threatpost.com/?=medical

(Canada) The Globe and Mail, Thursday Oct. 27, 2011, Jim Finkle. "Insulin Pumps Vulnerable to Attacks by Hackers."

Medical Device guidelines (EU):

http://ec.europa.eu/enterprise/sectors/medical-devices/documents/guidelines/index_en.htm

http://www.forbes.com/sites/ericbasu/2013/08/03/hacking-insulin-pumps-and-other-medical-devices-reality-not-fiction/

Jack, Barnaby "Implantable Medical Devices: Hacking Humans" presents at Black Hat USA Conference July 27-Aug 1, 2013, Caesars Palace, Las Vegas, Nevada.

Wallace, Delores R. and Kuhn, D. Richard, "Lessons from 342 Medical Device Failures," Information Technology Laboratory, National Institute of Standards and Technology,

http://www.cbsnews.com/news/when-medical-implants-fail/

http://www.propublica.org/special/four-medical-implants-that-escaped-fda-scrutiny

### Vaccines

You can also be a member of the small group for which certain vaccines are dangerous or fatal. This is such a large sample set that specialized "vaccine injury lawyers" have evolved. It has even trigger an anti-vaccine movement. There is statistical proof that vaccines do more good than harm, but they are not perfect. There is even a "Vaccine Adverse Event Reporting System (VAERS), created in 1990.

http://www.cdc.gov/vaccinesafety/ensuringsafety/monitoring/vaers/index.html

Any one can (and is encouraged to) report an adverse reaction to a vaccine, and they has been set up a National Vaccine Injury Compensation Program in the U. S. From the nearly 30,000 report submitted per year, a small percentage are classified as dangerous, meaning "adverse event resulted in permanent disability, hospitalization, life-threatening illness, or death. " The database serves as an early warning system for potential vaccine problems.

It has been found that, although problems have been seen after certain vaccinations, they are rarely caused by the vaccinations themselves.

A counter-example is the case that  American David Salamone and Jacob McCarthy from Australia both developed paralytic polio from the oral polio vaccine, which is no longer administered in the United States or Australia. Saba Button from Australia developed brain damage after ongoing febrile seizures from CSL's FluVax.

# Miscellaneous

"...but it worked last week..." Anon.

This sections contains  case studies that didn't fit anywhere else. I did not discuss the Nuclear Power Plant accidents at Chernobyl, 3 Miles Island, and Fukushima, as theses have been well-covered and analyzed.

## Death and injury by Safety Gear

Safety gear and Personal Protective Equipment is meant to step in when we encounter a dangerous situation. Sometimes it doesn't work like that.

In 2010, a New Zealand teenage girl was driving a mini-stock car on a track at the Kaikohe Speedway at a sponsored event. Unfortunately, she crashed into a barrier, and died of her injuries. She was wearing the specified driver safety equipment, including a helmet and neck brace. According to the Coroner, the adult-size helmet and brace were a contributing factor in her death.

Reference

"Speedway death followed by chaos," 24 Sept, 2013, www.3news.co.nz

In the early days of air bags in cars, people were injured by their activation. The manufacturers finally got the deployment speed correct. I will mention that my personal experience with air bag deployment was positive. Early accidents included having the car's windows blow out due to the deployment. A real fear is the false positive deployment which can certainly be a distraction to the driver. All-in-all, air bags have been shown to save lives and reduce injuries, but they are not completely fool-proof.

Another problem was seen in the use of fire suppressants in large computer rooms. You certainly don't want to use water, so systems were developed to flood the room with an inert gas instead. That's a good idea, except you had to remember to get all the people out first...

## Big Bay Boom

This was an incident at the Independence Day fireworks display in San Diego, California, July 4, 2012. Seven thousand fireworks, on 4 barges and a pier, went off simultaneously, instead of being sequenced over 17 minutes. There were ½ million viewers. This event lead to no injuries, but did result in over four million YouTube views of the video.

There was a primary launch file and a secondary back-up in the controlling computer. The two files were merged to create a new launch file, and sent to each of the five fireworks locations. Somehow, an "unintentional procedural step" happened in that process, causing an "anomaly" that doubled the primary firing sequence, the report said."

"The command code was initiated, and the 'new' file did exactly what it 'thought' it was supposed to do," the report says. "It executed all sequences simultaneously because the new primary file contained two sets of instructions. It executed the file we designed as well as the file that was created in the back-up downloading process."

Actually, I witnessed the same thing on the Fourth of July as a boy in my hometown. In that case, the the first manually launched fireworks (involving a man with a match) went short and hit the trailer where the rest of the fireworks were stored. It was spectacular but brief, the best ever. No one was hurt.

Reference

http://www.bigbayboom.com

## Dive Computer

A wrist mounted dive computer is a great thing for scuba enthusiasts. It will keep track of how long you have been at what depth, and advise you about stopping on the way back to the surface to let the nitrogen dissolved in the blood dissipate. Not doing this at the right time and for the right time can cause that painful condition known as "the bends." This is where the nitrogen in the bloodstream collects in the joints, and exert pressure. Another issue, called by divers the "martinni effect," is a nitrogen induced drunken state at depth. Automate the process, and make it safer. You don't need to read the depth meter and the elapsed time, and consult a chart. What could possibly go wrong?

A dive computer from Uwatec called the Aladin Air X Nitrox had an issue, undiscovered for 7 years.

The Dive computer provided incorrect information on safe dive and depth limits, leading to diver injury. The problem was shown to be a software defect that caused blood nitrogen levels to be underestimated. This occurred in a series of closely spaced dives, when there was not enough time between dives to allow all of the dissolved nitrogen to be removed from the bloodstream. Another problem was taking a plane flight too soon after diving. This caused the dissolved nitrogen that would have been no problem at sea level to be a big problem at altitude. In many cases, the bends, even when treated, cause permanent damage.

The biggest problem was the corporate cover-up that ensued when the manufacturer was made aware of the problem. This eventually lead to an investigation by the Consumer Product Safety Commission. The case went to Federal Court in 2001, and the product was recalled.

Reference

*The Risks Digest*, ACM Committee on Computers and Public Policy, Vol. 22, Issue 57, February 19, 2003.

## *FDIV*

The floating point divide error in the Intel P5 Pentium processor evaded Intel's testing and user notice, until a Professor of Mathematics at Lynchburg College in Virginia, Thomas R. Nicely, noticed some inconsistencies in his calculations in October of 1994. He documented the cases and notified Intel. How many billions of financial and scientific/engineering calculations had been done with this chip previously, and the results accepted as good?

Intel had actually been aware of the problem since May, based on testing of the next generation chip, the Pentium Pro. Intel decided not to change the chip design, as the error was seen as minor, and the changing of the chip was an expensive and time consuming process. The problem gained widespread attention after a CNN report, and many computer users went back to double-check their calculations.

There was a large public outcry, and Intel agreed to replace the flawed chips upon request. This had a significant impact on Intel's bottom line, the company claiming $475 million. The problem was attributed to a error in a look-up table on the chip.

The problem can be demonstrated on Pentium's of clock speed 66 MHz or less, by doing the calculation 4195835/3145727. The correct answer is

1.333820449136241002, but the chip will tell you its 1.33739068902037589. That's close enough, right? My H-P calculator says 1.33382045. My slide rule says 1.33.

So, what was designed based on errors in the calculations? What financial calculations were effected? Small error multiplied by a billion equals...

Reference

Wolfe, Alexander, "Intel fixes a Pentium FPU glitch," Electronic Engineering Times, Nov. 7, 1994.

www.trnicely.net/#PENT

## *Extinction Event*

An extinction event is defined as "a widespread and rapid decrease in the amount of life on Earth." Given that over 98% of the species we know of are extinct, we need to be careful with the home planet. There have been several mass extinctions on Earth since life began, none because of us. So far.

The most recent event was 66 million years ago. It is thought that this was caused by a asteroid hit. Large asteroid hits can cause mega-tsunamis and global forest fires. It may be the case, although currently unproven, that the meteor strike that created the Gulf of Mexico also caused the extinction of the dinosaurs.

The worst case, the Permian–Triassic extinction event, 250 million years ago, is estimated to have killed off over 90% of species

Ok, so the survival probability of the dinosaurs was shown to be low for large asteroid impacts. We're smarter than the dinosaurs though. Right?

In 1908, there was an air burst of a small asteroid over a remote location near Tunguska in Siberia. It was possibly the equivalent of a 30 megaton bomb, but it produced no crater. It is estimated that 80 million trees over an area of more than 2,000 square kilometers were destroyed. The ensuing shock wave measured 5 on the Richter scale. There were eye witnesses to the event. The first expedition to the site arrived some 10 years later. If the incident had occurred over a populated area, the result would have been total annihilation and mass causalities. Didn't see that one coming. But we have better detection systems now, right?

A similar yet smaller event occurred over a populated area in Russia near dawn on February 15, 2013, at Chelyabinsk in the Ural district of Russia,. It caused over 1,200 injuries, mainly from broken glass falling from windows shattered by the shock wave. It was a total surprise, and the immediate reaction was that it had to be a nuclear first strike by the United States. It turned out to be a 10,000 ton superbolide meteor, traveling at 34,000 mph over the Urals, and exploding around 25 kilometers over the surface. There was a bright flash and a shock wave, with a subsequent shower of fragments reaching the ground. Didn't see that one coming either.

Both professional astronomers and amateurs scan the nigh skies for potential threats. At the moment, we can't do much about it. The Chelyabinsk incident was interesting, as it came out of the rising sun, with no warning at all. The damage and death toll to a major city would have unimaginable.

References

Rubtsov, Vladimir; Ashpole, Edward *The Tunguska Mystery* (Astronomers' Universe) Copernicus; 2009 ed, 2010, Amazon Digital Services, Inc. ASIN: B008BAGYTC.

Marcos, C.; Marcos R. *The Chelyabinsk Superbolide: we didn't see that one coming,* The Baetylus Press; 1stt ed, 2013, Amazon Digital Services, Inc. ASIN: B00GWWCKK8 .

## Carrington Event

A large solar flare occurred in September of 1859, and was observed by British astronomer R. C. Carrington in his private observatory on his estate outside of London. Both the associated sunspots and the flare were visible to the naked eye. The resulting geomagnetic storm was recorded by a magnetograph in Britain as well. They also recorded a perturbation in the Earth's ionosphere, that we now know is caused by ionizing x-rays. In 1859, this was all observed, but not understood. Even the ionosphere was not know to exist at the time. Now, we know a Coronal Mass Ejection from the sun, associated with a solar storm, is first seen as an energy burst hitting the Earth, and later by vast streams of charged particles, that travel slower than the speed of light. At normal levels, these particles are seen as the Northern or Southern lights. The Earth's magnetic filed is affected.

What did happen, and was not immediately associated with the solar storm, was interference with the early telegraph systems of the time. The telegraph was relatively new, and wires stretched for many miles. Think of them as long antennas. The telegraph equipment was damaged, and large arc's of electricity started fires and shocked operators. No fatalities were reported. The employees of American Telegraph Company in New York found they could transmit messages with the batteries of their systems disconnected. The Northern lights were visible from Cuba. This was the largest such solar flare in at least 500 years...and so far.

What if such a super flare occurred today? First, we would have warning from sentinel satellites such as the Solar Dynamics Observatory, that are closer to the sun, and detect the passage of particles. They can tell us about this via radio, which travels faster than the particles. So, we would have a day or so's notice. All of our modern high-technology infrastructure would be at risk of damage, from the electrical grid to the Internet. Most of our satellites would be damaged, removing services we rely on such as long distance data communication, and navigation. It would be much better to turn everything off, and ride out the storm. Even that might not prevent major damage to networks. When is the next large solar event? Even the Astrophysicists can't tell us that. Only that it will eventually occur. Stay tuned...

Reference

http://www.history.com/news/a-perfect-solar-superstorm-the-1859-carrington-event

Standage, Tom *The Victorian Internet: The Remarkable Story of the Telegraph and the Nineteenth Century's On-Line Pioneers,* Walker & Company; 1st ed, 1998, ISBN-:0802713424.

# Tsunami

There you are, sitting on the beach, enjoying yourself, when you notice a small incoming continuous wave, something like a rising tide. This is caused by a seismic event out to sea. In the open water, the height of the wave you hardly be noticed. As it approaches land, it builds up as the ocean floor rises. Tsunami is the Japanese word for harbor wave. They have much longer wavelengths than normal ocean waves. They were known to the 5th century b.c. Greeks.

In 2004, and Indian Ocean tsunami was among the deadliest natural disasters in human history with at least 230,000 people killed or missing in 14 countries. Before that, the 1755 Lisbon earthquake and tsunami had caused thousands of deaths, and massive destruction. In 1908, a tsunami caused nearly 125,000 deaths in Sicily and nearby areas.

And, then there's the mega-tsunami. These could in theory cross an ocean, but have not yet been observed. Tsunami's can also occur in fresh water lakes.

The Fukushima Daiichi nuclear disaster was directly triggered by an earthquake and tsunami, when waves exceeded the height of the plant's sea wall. The area, known to be at high risk from tsunami, had tsunami barriers walls totaling 25 kilometres long (but not high enough). The 2011 tsunami toppled more than 50% of the walls and caused catastrophic damage

# Afterword

Well, the answer is, there's a lot that can go wrong, even in the simplest cases. Systems are designed by humans, and humans are fallible. We can reduce the probably of failure, but we can't completely eliminate it. To err is human, they say, to really screw things up requires a computer.

There was a lot of material to choose from in pulling this book together. I didn't want to go to extremes, so I left out a lot detail of well know cases: the eruption of the volcano Krakatoa, the "Year without a summer," the Big Northeast Blackout, and many more. You don't need to look far to find similar stories. There's a lot more material relating to incidents that occurred since this book came out. Are we getting any smarter, and more ready? Sleep well.

If you're now curled up in an underground bunker in the fetal position, you missed the point of the book. We can influence systems, we can plan for contingencies, we can learn the lessons of the past and apply them.

If you really want to see the worst that can happen, see the movie, "The Martian."

# Glossary

Ada – a software language

AFB – Air Force base.

APU – auxiliary power unit.

Bends – a painful condition, resulting from the nitrogen dissolved in the blood stream collecting in the joints,

Blue Screen of Death – an error page in the Windows operating System

Buran – the Russian space shuttle.

CDC – (U. S.) Centers for Disease Control

CME – Coronal Mass Ejection on the Sun

Cntrl-Alt-Del – the three key combination used to reset a pc; developed by IBM to intentionally be difficult to do accidentally; sometimes called the three-fingered salute.

CPSC – U. S. Consumer Product Safety Commission.

CPU – central processing unit (computer)

Cyber-terrorism – terrorist acts committed over the Internet.

Duplicate – provide two solutions

Error segmentation – keeping the effects of an error from cascading.

EVA – extra-vehicular activity; going outside the spacecraft.

FAA – (U.S.) Federal Aviation Administration.

Fail-safe – a failure does not cause a fault.

Fault Tolerant – a property of a system where 1 or more faults won't cause it to fail.

Fault Tree – a graphical representation of faults and causes.

FDA – (U. S.) Food & Drug Administration.

FDIV – floating point divide operation

Firewall – a computer that connects a local computer to a wider network, and provides protection.

Flash – a non-volatile memory, like in flash-drives.

Flight Software – software used onboard space missions.

Floating point – a computer number format, like scientific notation.

FMEA – Failure Modes and Effects Analysis.

GAO – (U. S.) General Accounting Office.

Hubris – from the Greek, extreme pride or self-confidence; sometimes found in engineering design.

Hypergolic - components spontaneously ignite when they come into contact with each other.

IRBM – intermediate range ballistic missile.

ISS – International Space Station.

IV&V – independent verification and validation – having some one else look over the system

MIR – Russian space station; since reentered the atmosphere.

LAN – local area network.

LLRV – lunar lander research vehicle (for Apollo)

LOCV – loss of crew and vehicle.

Malware – malicious software

MTBF – Mean time between failures

MTTF – Mean Time to failure.

MTTR – Mean time to Repair.

Mutex – a software mechanism to provide mutual exclusion in processes.

NASA – the U.S. Space agency

NFPA – U. S. National Fire Protection Association.

NTSB – (US) National Transportation Safety Board – responsible for accident investigations.

OAMS – Orbit and Attitude Maneuvering System, on the Gemini spacecraft.

Phobos-Grunt -Russian mission to sample-return from the Martian moon Phobos. Grunt = ground.

Pitot tube – device on an aircraft measuring speed via air pressure differences.

Plan B – what to resort to when Plan A fails.

Post mortem – investigation after the fact.

Priority Inversion – a condition in a real-time operating system, in which a high priority task is held up by a low priority task holding a key resource. Demonstrated on the surface of Mars.

RAD-6000 – a radiation hard space computer

RCA – Root Cause Analysis

Redundant – providing multiple units, either completely identical; or functionally identical.

Relay – electromagnetic switch

Reset – return to a know, initial condition.

RFNA – red fuming nitric acid, an oxydizer.

RoHS – restriction of hazardous substances.

Root cause - the first cause, the starting point of events.

Roscosmos – the Russian space agency

RPN – risk priority number, in a FMEA.

RS-6000 – older flight computer architecture.

Rush-hour – inappropriately named morning and evening event when traffic moves at a crawl.

Scud – a Russian ballistic missile

SI – System Internationale (metric)

Soyuz – Russian manned space capsule, still in use.

SRAM – static random access memory.

SRB – (Shuttle) solid rocket boosters

SSME – Space Shuttle Main Engine (liquid propellant).

Stall – condition in which there is not enough air moving over the wings of an aircraft, and it looses lift.

STS – Space Transportation System (Shuttle).

Third rail (3rd rail) – a power distribution system for subways.

Tram – a light rail system used for passenger service in cities. A bus on rails.

Triplicate – provide three solutions.

TPS – (Space shuttle) Thermal protection system – tiles.

UDMH - Unsymmetrical dimethylhydrazine, a rocket fuel. Hypergolic with nitrogen tetroxide.

VAB – Vertical Assembly Building at KSC. Used for Saturn and Shuttle assembly and test.

VAERS – CDC's Vaccine Adverse Event Reporting System

Voting logic – choose the majority, based on the assumption that 2 failures are less probable than one.

VxWorks – a real time operating systems from Wind River Systems.

Zombie-Sat – out-of-control non-responsive satellite posing a danger to other spacecraft.

# References

Berk, Joseph *Systems Failure Analysis*, ASM International, November 17, 2009, ISBN-1615030123.

Bible, George *Train Wreck: The Forensics of Rail Disasters,* Johns Hopkins University Press , 2012, ASIN: B0099SKJXW.

Bozzano, Marco and Villafiorita, Adolfo *Design and Safety Assessment of Critical Systems*, Auerbach Publications; 1st edition, November 12, 2010, ISBN-1439803315.

Burgess, Colin; Kate Doolan, Kate;  Vis, Bert F*allen Astronauts: Heroes Who Died Reaching for the Moon*, 2003, Bison Books, ISBN-0803262124.

Burrough, Bryan *Dragonfly: NASA and the Crisis Aboard Mir,* 1998, 1$^{st}$ ed, HarperCollins, ISBN-0887307833.

Burrough, Bryan *Dragonfly: The Terrifying Story of Mir, Earth's First Outpost in Space,* 1999, fourth Estate Ltd. ISBN-1841150886.

Burrough, Bryan *Dragonfly: An Epic Adventure of Survival in Outer Space,* Harper Perennial; reprint edition, march 1, 2000, ASIN-B010EW4GMQ.

Charette, Robert N. "Air France Flight 447 Crash Causes in Part Point to Automation Paradox," July 10, 2012, http://spectrum.ieee.org.

Cheng, P.G. 100 *Questions for Technical Review,* Aerospace Report No. TOR-2005(8617)-4204. Space and Missile Systems Center. September 30, 2005.

Dunn William R. *Practical Design of Safety-Critical Computer Systems*, July 2002, ISBN-0971752702.

Durant, Will and Ariel, *The Lessons of History*, 1$^{st}$ ed, 1968, Simon & Schuster, ISBN- 143914995X.

Fawcett, Bill *100 Mistakes that Changed History: Backfires and Blunders That Collapsed Empires, Crashed Economies, and Altered th e Course of Our World,* Berkley, 2010, ASIN B0042JSOSA.

Fawcett, Bill *Trust Me, I Know What I'm Doing: 100 More Mistakes That Lost Elections, Ended Empires, and Made the World What It Is Today,* Berkley, 2013, ISBN-0425257363.

Fowler, Kim *Mission-Critical and Safety-Critical Systems Handbook: Design and Development for Embedded Applications* Newnes; 1st edition, November 20, 2009, ISBN- 0750685670.

Gill, Paul S. ; Garcia, Danny *Engineering Lessons Learned and Systems Engineering Applications,* NASA

  https://www.researchgate.net/publication/242185667_Engineering_Lessons_Learned_and_Systems_Engineering_Applications

Harland, David M. and Lorentz, Ralph D. *Space Systems Failures, Disasters and Rescues of Satellites, Rockets and Space Probes*, Springer, 2005, ISBN 0-387-21519-0.

Hermann, Debra S. *Software Safety and Reliability: Techniques, Approaches, and Standards of Key Industrial Sectors*, Wiley-IEEE Computer Society Press; 1st edition, February 10, 2000, ISBN0769502997.

Hobbs, Chris *Embedded Software Development for Safety Critical Systems*, Auerbach Publications, 2015, ISBN-1498726704.

Jones, Capers *Patterns of Software System Failure and Success*, International Thomson Computer Press (December 1995), ISBN-10: 1850328048.

Kichenside, Geoffrey *Great Train Disasters: The World's Worst Railway Accidents*, 1997, Parragon Plus, ISBN-10: 0752522299.

Kieffer, Susan W. *The Dynamics of Disaster*, W. W. Norton & Company, 2013, ASIN: B007Q6XLHK.

Kalinsky, David "Architecture of safety-critical systems, 2005, http://www.embedded.com/design/prototyping-and-development/4006464/Architecture-of-safety-critical-systems#

Klotz, Irene "Programming Error Doomed Russian Mars Probe," Feb. 7, 2012, http://news.discovery.com/space/

Krämer, Bernd J. and Völker, Norbert (Eds.) *Safety-Critical Real-Time Systems*, December 3, 2010, ISBN-1441950192.

Krantz, Gene (2001). *Failure Is Not an Option: Mission Control from Mercury to Apollo 13 and Beyond,* New York: Simon & Shuster. ISBN 978-0-7432-0079-0.

Leveson, Nancy G. "Software Safety in Embedded Computer Systems," Communications of the ACM. Vol. 34, No. 2, February 1991. pp. 34-46.

Leveson, Nancy G. *System Safety and Computers*, Addison-Wesley, 1995, ISBN 0-201-11972-2.

Leveson, Nancy G. Engineering a Safer World: Systems Thinking Applied to Safety, The MIT Press, January 13, 2012, ISBN- 0262016621.

Linenger, Jerry M. *Letters from Mir,2003, McGraw-Hill, ISBN-0-07-140009-5.*

Lochbaum, David; Edwin Lyman, Edwin; Stranahan, Susan Q. *Fukushima: The Story of a Nuclear Disaster, The New Press, 2014, ASIN: B00EXCAJKC, ISBN: 1595589082.*

Petroski, Henry *To Forgive Design: Understanding Failure*, Belknap Press of Harvard University Press (March 30, 2012), ISBN-10: 0674065840.

Petroski, Henry *To Engineer Is Human: The Role of Failure in Successful Design*, Vintage, 1992, ISBN-10: 0679734163.

Petroski, Henry *Success through Failure: The Paradox of Design* Vintage, 1992, ISBN-10: 0679734163.

Schlager, Neil (Ed) *When Technology Fails: Significant Technological Disasters, Accidents, and Failures of the Twentieth Century*, Gale Research (1994), ISBN-10: 0810389088.

Spark, Nick T. *A History of Murphy's Law,"* Periscope Film, 2006, ISBN 0-9786388-9-1.

Storey, Neil *Safety-Critical Computer Systems*, Addison-Wesley, 1996. ISBN: 0-201-42787-7.

Turtledove, Harry, Supervolcano: Eruption (Novel), Roc; Reprint edition, 2011, Penguin Group (USA) LLC, ISBN: 0451464206, ASIN B005ERIKF6.

Vogel, David A. *Medical Device Software Verification, Validation and Compliance* Artech House; November 30, 2010, ISBN- 1596934220.

Wallis, L. A., Greaves, I *Injuries Associated with Airbag Deployment, Emerg Med J 2002;19:490-493 doi:10.1136/emj.19.6.490.*

Wichmann, Brian A. Software in Safety Related Systems, Wiley, 1992. ISBN: 0471-93474-7.

"Air Traffic Control Computer Failures: Hearings before a subcommittee of the Committee on Government Operations, House of Representatives, second session, June 30 and August 15, 1980," University of Michigan Library 1980, ASIN: B00300GEMK.

NASA Better Mechanisms Needed for Sharing Lessons Learned, January 2002, United States Government Accounting Office, Report to the Subcommittee on Space and Aeronautics, committee on Science, House of Representatives, GAO-02-195.

Material from Wikipedia (www.wikipedia.org) is used under the conditions of the Creative Commons Attribution-ShareAlike #.0 Unported License.

Useful websites

National Transportation Safety Board, https://www/ntsb.gov

Consumer Product Safety Commission, www.cpsc.gov

National Fire Protection Association, www.nfpa.org

http://www.space.com/10694-human-spaceflight-dangers-infographic.html

Levenson, Nancy *sunnyday.mit.edu/accidents/*

http://www.embedded.com/columns/technicalinsights/169600396.

This is the website for a new series on the Science Channel that has some fairly well research and well presented space-realated disasters:

http://www.sciencechannel.com/tv-shows/secret-space-escapes/

http://www.iflscience.com/5-most-hair-raising-moments-history-spaceflight

http://www.spacesafetymagazine.com/space-disasters/

If you enjoyed this book, you might find something else from the author interesting as well. Available on Amazon Kindle.

Computer Architecture

4- and 8-bit Microprocessors, Architecture and History.

16-bit Microprocessors, History and Architecture.

RISC Microprocessors, History and Overview.

Floating Point Computation.

Computer Architecture and Programming of the Intel X86 Family.

The Hardware and Software Architecture of the Transputer .

The Architecture and Applications of the ARM Microprocessors.

Embedded Computer Systems, Vol. 1, Introduction and Architecture.

Embedded Computer Systems, Vol. 2, Implementing Embedded (Fall, 2015)

Architecture of Massively Parallel Microprocessor Systems.

Computer Virtualization and the Cloud.

Multicore Computer Architectures

Mainframes (Summer 2015)

Microprocessors in Space

The History of Spacecraft Computers from the V-2 to the Space Station

The Saturn Rocket and the Pegasus Missions.

Robots and Telerobots in Space Applications.

Microprocessors in Space

Apollo's Computers.

Personal Robots.

Earth Rovers: for Exploration and Environmental Monitoring.

Robots and Telerobots in Space Applications.

www.ingramcontent.com/pod-product-compliance
Lightning Source LLC
Chambersburg PA
CBHW050502290526
45786CB00006B/2406